BROADWAY BOOKS | NEW YORK

THE

ITTY BITTY KITCHEN

HANDBOOK

**EVERYTHING
YOU NEED TO KNOW ABOUT
SETTING UP & COOKING IN
THE MOST**

Ridiculously

**SMALL KITCHEN IN THE WORLD—
YOUR OWN**

Justin Spring

ILLUSTRATIONS BY JOEL HOLLAND

PRINTED IN THE UNITED STATES OF AMERICA

BROADWAY BOOKS and its logo, a letter B bisected on the
diagonal, are trademarks of Random House, Inc.

Visit our Web site at www.broadwaybooks.com

First edition published 2006

Book design by Elizabeth Rendfleisch

Library of Congress Cataloging-in-Publication Data

Spring, Justin.
    The itty bitty kitchen handbook : everything you need to
know about setting up & cooking in the most ridiculously small
kitchen in the world—your own / Justin Spring.— 1st ed.
        p. cm.
    Includes index.
    1. Cookery. 2. Kitchens. I. Title.

TX652.S64 2006
641.5—dc22   2005046959

ISBN 0-7679-2016-3

10 9 8 7 6 5 4 3 2 1

for Mom
who teaches by example

Happy Birthday
June 24, 2015
Love
mama

Contents

ACKNOWLEDGMENTS

All my friends had enthusiastic and helpful suggestions for this book, both in and out of the kitchen. But I would specifically like to thank Lucia Guimaraes, Pier Gustafson, Sharon Johe, Anthony Korner, Edward de Luca, Francine Maroukian, Chris and Danielle McConnell, Rosalind Pierce Spring, George Shackleford, Luciana Souza, and Jim Zajac for their interest in the project—most especially Francine Maroukian, who was so supportive (and wise) from the very first moment. A special thanks, as well, to professional organizer Ilene Drexler of The Organizing Wiz. I would also like to thank my agent, Charlotte Sheedy, and my editor, Jennifer Josephy, for all their helpful comments and advice on the manuscript, which really did come a long way under their guidance. And I would like to thank those supremely gifted writer-cooks whose work inspired me to develop a number of the small-kitchen recipes in this book: James Beard, Marion Rombauer Becker, Mark Bittman, Peg Bracken, Julia Child, Marcella Hazan, Michael McLaughlin, Jacques Pépin, Delia Smith, and Horst Scharfenberg. Last but not least, I would like to thank my kitchen companion, silent partner, and recipe-tester of the past thirteen years—my basset hound, Lovey.

Do it simply.

—ESCOFFIER (!)

THE
ITTY BITTY KITCHEN
HANDBOOK

*H*orrified BY THE SIZE OF YOUR KITCHEN? YOU'RE NOT ALONE. MANY APARTMENTS TODAY FEATURE KITCHENS SHRUNK INTO NOOKS, INSTALLED IN FORMER COAT CLOSETS, OR ELSE SIMPLY OMITTED ALTOGETHER TO "MAXIMIZE" OUR LIVING SPACE. LITTLE WONDER, THEN, THAT EVEN THOSE OF US IN SMALL HOMES WHO LOVE THE *IDEA* OF COOKING PREFER WATCHING IT ON TELEVISION OR READING ABOUT IT IN MAGAZINES TO ACTUALLY GRAPPLING WITH IT IN REAL TIME IN OUR OWN ITTY BITTY KITCHENS.

BUT COOKING IN IMPOSSIBLY TINY SPACES IS HARDLY A NEW IDEA. ASTRONAUTS, STEWARDESSES, AND PULLMAN PORTERS HAVE LONG KNOWN THE DUBIOUS PLEASURE OF PREPARING MEALS (SOMETIMES BY THE HUNDREDS) IN SPACES THE SIZE OF A PHONE BOOTH. MUCH OF THE most brilliant cooking in the world gets done in restaurant kitchens no larger than the kitchen of a studio apartment. People living aboard sailboats or in recreational vehicles, meanwhile, routinely cook larger meals under much less agreeable conditions than those of the average apartment dweller. And anyone who has ever visited Paris has probably gasped at what passes for a domestic kitchen in that world capital of gastronomy.

What is new to our generation is the expectation that we can cook in an absurdly limited, awkward space on doll-sized appliances *and actually enjoy the activity as a form of domestic recreation*. Which is not, of course, to say that it can't be enjoyed: Cooking is always a creative adventure, full of suspense regarding the success or failure of our experiments, resulting almost always in sensual satisfaction, physical fulfillment, and incidental merriment. But it isn't always easy or blissful to cook in the small, awkward spaces in which many of us find ourselves, alone and with can opener in hand, at the end of a long and stressful day.

Whatever your lifestyle is, whatever your culinary fantasies may be, you probably already know that improvisational small-space cooking is much more complicated than "regular" cooking, not only because the available options and resources are so much more limited, but also because (let's face it) the instinctual response to any small, hot, crowded, messy, and potentially dangerous area of confinement is not so much pleasure as claustrophobic panic. Cooking well in a tight space therefore requires not only patience, agility, and forethought, but also, most important, a well-developed ability to *simply chill out*. In that sense, it is something like taking a berth on *Das Boot:* Some of us are well suited to the job, temperamentally; others are just bound to crack.

It's easy to laugh about itty bitty kitchens, because the idea of *loving* to spend time in a stifling, anxiety-ridden, and poorly designed cooking space is nothing if not absurd. But the extreme limitation of the itty bitty kitchen also invites us to reconsider just what cooking is and how it must get done—which is to say, it allows us a certain leeway in our small-space practice of the culinary arts.

This handbook for itty bitty kitchens attempts to close the gap between the kitchens we have and the cooking we wish we could do by giving readers not only some seriously helpful information on kitchen organization but also some really good cooking shortcuts and cheating methods. Through smart shopping, a well-organized kitchen, and an appropriate sense of what's *actually* possible, you really can develop a knack for making good, solid meals in your tiny little kitchen—and have a pretty good time doing it. I know this to be so, because I have done it for over a decade.

The first part of this book will help you organize, streamline, and optimize your itty bitty kitchen. The second part will suggest some new ways to make meals (and stay sane) once you've got that tiny little kitchen of yours all set up and provisioned for cooking.

But (lest you think otherwise) this is not a book for the overly ambitious: The pages ahead do not suggest expensive kitchen renovations or elaborate meal plans. Instead, it's a book based on the very simple kitchen I have organized and worked in for the past twelve years (a space of forty-five square feet) and also, to some degree, on the small, thirty-six-foot sailboat on which I spent weekends, vacations, and summers while growing up. As a result, the book offers a good deal of hard-won advice that will seem relatively dopey to those inhabiting larger kitchen spaces, but which will nonetheless be really, really useful to those of us with super-small ones.

The recipes may likewise seem a bit basic to people who like cooking that showcases exotic ingredients and requires elaborate cooking techniques, but they will prove very handy to those of us with a taste for simple cooking who are coping with ultra-small kitchens, minimal appliances, and busy schedules. Think of it, if you like, as Boy-Scout-type cooking, only substituting two burners and a toaster oven for the campfire.

In the first half of this book we'll coax your troubled little kitchen into being all it can be. Since clutter is particularly toxic to small kitchen spaces, we'll start with some purging (and even get a little touchy-feely about why it's so hard to keep a kitchen clutter free), then move on to deep cleaning and organizing. We'll optimize your appliances, sort through your cabinets to minimize disorganization and confusion, and then review ways to brighten and improve the place—since the nicer your little kitchen is, the more inclined you'll be to *actually* spend time in it.

The second half of the book will demonstrate how to turn groceries into meals when working in a very small space. It will lay out some simple ideas for fast dinners, from single-serving items to cold plates to big-batch recipes that will enable you, during moments of supreme ambition (or else procrastination), to make a great big pot of food that can be either eaten all at once at a dinner party or else frozen in portions for easily reheated one- or two-person meals. Incidentally, since some people's kitchens are *very small indeed,* I have selected recipes that can be cooked using nothing more than a stovetop, hot plate, or moderate-size toaster oven, employing an equally limited number of dishes and utensils. I have also emphasized foods that store and reheat well, since it's always nice to have some good, dependable ready-cooked food waiting in the fridge instead of starting from scratch every time.

After the recipes section, we'll briefly consider the prickly little question of how to hold a dinner party in a small space with a very small kitchen. We will then move on to a chapter on how to keep your little kitchen perfectly neat and functional between mealtimes, since cleanliness and order are so absolutely necessary to successfully managing a small kitchen (and a small home).

The key to cooking and maintaining an impossibly tiny kitchen (whether at sea, on wheels, or in the middle of a space-challenged city) is in setting up your kitchen so that with minimum effort you get maximum results. Sometimes it's fun to cook, and sometimes it isn't; some things are easier to cook, and some things are harder; some places are really fun to cook in, and other places are, well, very much less so. The itty bitty kitchen is a more challenging place than most, and it requires above-average patience and ingenuity from its cook. But with the right attitude, a little thoughtful preparation, and a shameless inclination to cut corners at every conceivable opportunity, you're going to create some really great meals here. And when that food finally *does* hit the table, you'll have won some hard-earned bragging rights, too—because, after all, you made it in your *itty bitty* kitchen.

PART 1

ORDER IN THE
ITTY BITTY KITCHEN

1

*O*ne OF THE MOST SURPRISING THINGS ABOUT PRESIDING OVER A FUNCTIONAL SMALL KITCHEN IS DISCOVERING HOW FEW THINGS YOU ACTUALLY NEED IN ORDER TO ACCOMPLISH THE MAJORITY OF YOUR COOKING TASKS—AND HOW CREATIVELY YOU CAN IMPROVISE WHEN YOU HAVEN'T GOT MUCH SPECIAL EQUIPMENT. ANOTHER EQUALLY SURPRISING THING ABOUT YOUR FUNCTIONAL SMALL KITCHEN IS THAT IT BECOMES INCREASINGLY *DYS*FUNCTIONAL AS IT FILLS UP WITH THINGS THAT ARE, ON FIRST APPEARANCE, QUITE USEFUL—TO THE POINT THAT, CRAMMED FULL OF GREAT **STUFF**, IT BECOMES ALMOST ENTIRELY UNUSABLE.

SO, IF YOU'RE JUST MOVING IN TO YOUR NEW APARTMENT, DON'T UNPACK THOSE BOXES MARKED "KITCHEN" JUST YET. INSTEAD, STOP FOR a moment and consider your barren little kitchen as it now exists—pristine, empty, and full of potential. You have shelf space, drawer space, and counter space. So . . . if your boxes contain things you don't really want and hardly ever use, things that up until now you haven't had the energy, focus, or drive to throw out (in other words, **STUFF**), consider leaving it all boxed up for a while.

Now visualize cooking in a tiny kitchen of Zen-garden simplicity (do you hear the distant strains of a shakuhachi flute?)—a place that holds the absolute minimum of objects, in which you still have room enough to cook.

This, too, can be yours.

For Those Who Have Just Arrived in a New Home

IF YOU ARE JUST MOVING IN TO YOUR NEW KITCHEN, try the following experiment. Rather than unpack your kitchen boxes, leave them as is, and instead take things out of them on an as needed basis. Once you have used something, find a place for it in your kitchen cabinets.

Over the course of the next two weeks, you are going to discover how many things—plates, cups, glasses, silverware, pots, pans—you *actually* use. At the end of that time, if you dare, consider putting all the rest of your **STUFF** into storage.

Can you rise to the challenge? If you're like most people, you can't and you won't. So . . . read on.

George and His Royal Crown Derby: A Cautionary Tale

PROFESSIONAL ORGANIZERS ALL AGREE that the hardest and least glamorous part of reorganizing any kitchen is clearing it out so it can work properly—and also that the longer a person has lived in a space, the more cluttered his or her kitchen will have become. If you are not a natural-born thrower-outer (and few of us are), the hardest part of clearing out an object-filled kitchen is going to be in getting started, not only because you are basically conflicted about the need for change of any sort but also because you fear that removing even the smallest item will bring irrevocable loss.

Let's for a moment consider an extreme case: a museum curator named George. George lives in a five-hundred-square-foot apartment featuring a modest galley kitchen with six cabinets. He likes to cook, and when he first moved in to his apartment ten years back, his kitchen provided him with just enough cooking and storage space for entertaining friends with the simple home-cooked foods that every homesick, space-challenged, yet relentlessly cosmopolitan city dweller craves.

George's home life took a sudden turn for the worse, however, when his rich uncle Clayton died and left him a service for forty of Royal Crown Derby "Red Aves," an ornately patterned red-and-white china dating from the late 1930s featuring images of birds of paradise and oriental pheasants amid exquisitely detailed feathers and foliage. George already owned his own dishes—a perfectly nice set of Spode "Florentine" for ten (purchased both charitably and economically at the Lenox Hill Hospital Thrift Shop), plus several smaller sets of dessert plates and breakfast china picked up here and there on his assorted wanderings through Europe. But Clayton's "Red Aves" was *family* china. And so, with some juggling, George found a place in his kitchen cabinets for *all of it*. Of course, there was no longer any room there for his cookware, his utensils, or his food.

For a while, George managed to make an occasional meal, because he still loved cooking and entertaining. It was just a whole lot more complicated and frustrating to do so. But then his aunt Gladys, Clayton's sister, left George her monogrammed silver: Tiffany "Wave Edge," a combination luncheon and dinner service, also for forty (with related hollowware and buffet items), which she, in turn, had inherited from her parents. Since her monogram was George's monogram too, how could he say no?

A month later, entirely unannounced, four crates of monogrammed linens arrived via U-Haul, along with Aunt Gladys's cat.

That really was the end of George's kitchen.

Today, George no longer cooks. His kitchen and closets are so full of dishes and silver and linens that he pretty much

lives on take-out food. While he still loves to entertain, he does so these days in the most joyless and perfunctory of ways: by purchasing precooked meals at the supermarket, bypassing his kitchen entirely, and simply unpacking his rotisserie chicken and supermarket coleslaw right there at the dinner table. He nonetheless takes great pride in serving these cold, flavorless foods in high style—on the same gorgeous china, silver, and linens *that have otherwise ruined his life!*

Kitchen Clutter Intervention

IF, LIKE GEORGE, YOU ARE AN UNREPENTANT COLLECTOR OF STUFF, you are probably not going to clear out your itty bitty kitchen cabinets without what is known as a *therapeutic intervention*. An intervention happens when a concerned family member or friend steps forward to confront you with the news that you have a serious problem that is clearly interfering with your ability to function. In this case, your problem is kitchen-cluttering STUFF.

Your first step toward recovery will be in admitting that you are powerless over kitchen-cluttering STUFF, and that your kitchen life has become unmanageable as a result.

Your second step will be to envision your kitchen as once again a working kitchen, rather than just a storage area for STUFF.

Your third step will be to believe that, through the de-clutterizing process, your kitchen can be emptied of STUFF and restored to normal order and use—and also that, by extension, once this STUFF disappears, your life will be vastly improved by your newfound ability to make your kitchen function (that is, *to cook*).

Your fourth step, of course, is actually getting in to that kitchen and ridding it of **STUFF**.

Once you decide that a fully functional, **STUFF**-free kitchen is something you really want—and George, God bless him, may never get there—here is how you start.

The Art of the Purge

ORGANIZATION EXPERTS who consult with home owners on the management of domestic space have many approaches and techniques for getting a kitchen into shape, but all agree that the key to managing any space *well* is to rid it of **STUFF**. You can pay one of these highly effective consultants anywhere from fifty to two hundred dollars an hour to help you with the process—and it's a valuable service, costing less than psychotherapy; reach one of them through the National Association of Professional Organizers, www.napo.net, which has an automated online referral system. But a more economical alternative is simply to suck it up and do the work yourself. If you choose this latter course of action, you will need an extremely well-organized friend to stand in for that expensive, experienced, and totally focused professional organizer.

So select your mentor carefully. Someone who has himself conquered a clutter problem is best, since that person will know exactly what you are facing, and at the same time will have an appropriate (which is to say *limited*) sympathy for your anguish. Those who have mastered the art of home organization and STUFF removal are often keen to share their hard-won skills with others, but the skill itself is based on a "tough love" philosophy, for STUFF is infernally seductive; in fact, the STUFF of addiction.

Once you have found the right person to help you, here's the drill.

First, prepare by getting your kitchen as clean and neat as it can be. (Otherwise you may panic and give up.) You will have better luck with your kitchen purge if the rest of your little home is very clean too, since once you start unpacking your kitchen, STUFF is going to flood into your living space and threaten to take over your life.

Second, agree in advance that your well-organized friend will supervise you for a set period of time (four hours is about as much as most people can take). Don't hesitate to offer some kind of hourly payment or in-kind recompense for the job, since a "clock-is-ticking" mentality actually helps keep both of you motivated (the natural inclination, halfway through the job, is to wander away from the kitchen, pour a large cocktail, and watch some TV).

Now, with the help of this limited-sympathy friend, lay out five boxes or areas in the middle of your living space, labeling them as follows: PUT AWAY (KITCHEN), PUT AWAY (ELSEWHERE), GIVE AWAY/SELL, STORAGE, and TRASH. Now start sorting through your STUFF, putting each thing into one of the five boxes. Your friend's job is to urge you on, keep you from getting distracted, and correct you when you start putting huge amounts of STUFF back into the PUT AWAY (KITCHEN) box. He or she will also encourage you to stop sniveling and whining about what is, essentially, a whole lot of really useless junk.

Not everyone can do their entire kitchen in one go. If you are dealing with extreme amounts of STUFF, or find de-STUFFing your entire kitchen simply too overwhelming because of STUFF-related emotional distress, allow yourself to do the job gradually. Do one box, one cupboard, one drawer, or one shelf. But once you commit to spending a certain amount of time sorting and discarding, stick to it!

When you have finished all of your sorting for the day, hurry the box marked TRASH out the door. The GIVE AWAY/SELL box should also leave sooner rather than later—your stern but caring friend may even offer to take it away on your behalf (he'll probably try to sell it on eBay, but that's his business).

Remember, your kitchen is small, so even if it's packed full of STUFF, this will not be an endless task. Just remember that recovery from STUFF addiction is an ongoing process—a process you will return to, over and over again, for as long as you preside over a kitchen, itty bitty or otherwise.

For Those Who Can't Let Go: Some Tips and Tricks for Kitchen Pack Rats

LETTING GO OF STUFF comes easier to some than to others. For those of us who have a really hard time getting rid of unused and unneeded kitchen STUFF, here are some thoughts to keep in mind:

1. Remember that much of the STUFF you are now going to make a decision about was in fact given to you by someone who, however thrifty, secretly wanted to be rid of it—and finessed the job by giving it *to you*.

2. Console yourself that much of the STUFF you are making decisions about was never meant to be held on to and has no great commercial value.

3. Beware of meaningless sentimental attachments.

4. Focus, whenever possible, on the possibility that by cleaning out your kitchen cabinets you will be giving some really good STUFF to others. Your guilt about letting go of STUFF (and your fear of unwittingly losing some really valuable STUFF) can thus be vanquished through the reassurance that you are *giving STUFF to charity*. Thrift shops that benefit specific charities are your best bet, since your STUFF will find a good home, the proceeds from the sale will help a worthy cause, and—hey!—you will even be getting a tax deduction.

5. Finally, and most important: remember that you are not so much *getting rid of STUFF* as *making room to live*.

2

*T*he NEXT STEP IN FINE-TUNING YOUR LITTLE KITCHEN WILL BE CLEANING IT. *REALLY* CLEANING IT. "WHY?" YOU ASK. WELL, SINCE PARED-DOWN AND FUNCTIONAL LITTLE WORK SPACES CAN'T REALLY BE "DECORATED," CLEANLINESS IS GOING TO BE WHAT PEOPLE IN THE DECORATING BIZ CALL "YOUR PRIMARY DESIGN STATEMENT."

SUPER-CLEANLINESS REALLY CAN MAKE EVEN THE HUMBLEST KITCHEN ENORMOUSLY ATTRACTIVE: IT'S A SIGN THAT THE PERSON WHO USES IT CARES PASSIONATELY ABOUT THE SPACE. SO BEGIN YOUR LIFE IN YOUR NEW KITCHEN WITH A SERIOUS SCOUR. DOING SO WILL INCIDENTALLY SERVE AS A GREAT INTRODUCTION TO YOUR WORK SPACE, FOR YOU WILL BECOME ACQUAINTED WITH ITS EVERY SQUARE INCH. IF YOU have any questions about how to clean, procrastinate by turning to Chapter 8 ("Cleanup Time: A Magnificent Obsession," page 204); otherwise, roll up your sleeves and read on.

Starting Out

THE FIRST ORDER OF THE DAY is to scrub everything thoroughly: refrigerator, freezer, oven, stovetop, countertops, sink, cabinets, and floor. Then scrub it again! In older, well-used, or downright decrepit kitchens, thin layers of vaporized grease will have accumulated and hardened onto every possible surface like some hellacious and ultra-nasty shellac. Special grease-stripping wall cleaners used by house-painters (such as trisodium phosphate, available commercially as Soilax) can be useful here. But good old-fashioned elbow grease can be equally effective.

Keep an eye out for signs of insect and animal life as you scrub. Remember that mice, should you have them, are best caught with glue traps, which (despite their "La Brea Tar Pits"–type spectacle of wild animals trapped in living death) are cheap, nontoxic, and highly effective at whisking away these offensive and disease-ridden creatures. Roaches and other pantry pests are best treated (at least at first) by an exterminator, who will diagnose the degree and source of your infestation, inspect your cabinetry for the cracks, holes, and crevices in which the pests hide and proliferate, seal the spaces up, and finish by giving you a whole lot of friendly advice on keeping your new kitchen pest free. When buying pesticides, remember to choose baits, bait stations, and gels (the best known and most effective of which are the Combat line of products by Clorox), since spray pesticides often cause allergic reactions and should never be used around food.

Next, if you have adjustable-height shelving, do a quick series of shelf-height checks: Are your food shelves arranged so that at least one of them can accommodate bottles standing upright? Are your dish shelves capable of accommodating your tallest glasses? If not, make your adjustments now, or prepare to face the consequences later.

Next, put down a smooth, washable, water-resistant shelf lining paper in the cupboards. In areas where you will store your glasses and plates, install breathable "waffle" or "ridged" liners, which will keep the plates and glasses from chipping or breaking if they fall, and at the same time improve air circulation, enabling them to dry even if put away slightly damp (which is certainly going to happen, because you have no other place in which to put them). In your undersink area, which will hold a number of strong and corrosive solvents, consider using peel-and-stick tiles instead of shelf paper to protect your cabinet flooring. Remember also that by placing hooks in all those little awkward spaces under the sink you can create storage for whisk brooms, dustpans and such like. (For more on under-sink storage, see page 40).

Fine-Tuning Appliances and Specialized Areas

NOW LET'S TAKE A MOMENT to assess how well your major appliances work, and whether you might add one or two small (but very useful!) appliances to your kitchen setup.

The Refrigerator

Consider washing out your refrigerator interior with a deodorizing solution of baking soda and water and (after unplugging the appliance) cleaning the coils on the back—they attract dust, which interferes with the refrigerator's ability to cool and thus drives up your energy costs. If the refrigerator has wire shelving inside, install sheets of Plexiglas over them—they will clean up easier, and your food items won't topple over so much. Just take the measurements to a hardware store and have the inexpensive Plexiglas cut to order.

Next, check the temperature. Refrigeration is optimal between 32 and 40 degrees Fahrenheit, while optimal freezer temperature is 0 degrees Fahrenheit (for those not good at math, that's 32 degrees *below* freezing). Food refrigeration is safest, spoilage slowest, in the lower range of refrigerator and freezer temperatures. But! You must balance your desire to keep your food safe from spoilage with your desire to keep it unfrozen. This can be tricky. The cooling dials within the refrigerator aren't always dependable, so the best way to eliminate the guesswork on temperature is by buying two inexpensive thermometers—one for the refrigerator, one for the freezer.

Available in most supermarkets for approximately $2 apiece, they have red marks indicating optimal refrigerator and freezer temperatures (thus are very easy to use) and come with clips that will attach easily to the railing inside the freezer or refrigerator doors (so you don't even have to worry about installing them). (A good example available online is the Taylor #5977 Refrigerator/Freezer thermometer, $2.99 at www.shop.com.)

The Oven

Should you be so blessed as to have a real oven in your IBK (yes, the space now merits an acronym!), give your prize appliance a thorough cleaning, then check the dials for wear. Illegible dials can usually be replaced very cheaply at your hardware superstore, as can rusty or unattractive burners. Nicks in oven (and refrigerator) porcelain can be touched up with an inexpensive porcelain repair kit. To streamline the look of your stovetop, purchase stainless-steel burner covers for less than $20. Both round (electric) and square (gas) burners are available at www.thegadgetsource.com and elsewhere; these covers can really make a difference in your kitchen's appearance, and they make cleanup easier, too. If you dislike scrubbing your oven, consider investing in a nonstick (Teflon) oven liner, available for less than $20 from the Chef's catalog (www.chefs catalog.com). A Teflon toaster-oven liner is less than $10 from the same source—and will come in very handy if your toaster oven lacks a removable crumb tray—but tinfoil works well here too, as any toasted-cheese sandwich addict will know.

Now test your oven for accuracy using an oven thermometer, because many ovens (expensive and otherwise) have faulty temperature settings. If the temperature is wildly inaccurate, have the oven calibrated; if it's only a little off (which is more likely), simply learn to make a manual adjustment, relying on your oven thermometer rather than the oven dial. While you're at it, try out that oven thermometer on your toaster oven too, since these smaller devices have tiny dials that can hardly be trusted for accuracy. (Incidentally, the two brand-new toaster ovens used in the writing and recipe-testing of this book—a Delonghi Alfredo Deluxe and a Krups ProChef—turned out to be 25 and 50 degrees off, respectively.)

What about the Microwave?

While many classically trained cooks hate microwave ovens, most small-apartment inhabitants find them indispensable. Today's microwave may still do bizarre things to an unattended piece of chicken, but it's also a compact, relatively foolproof, and inexpensive device—I nabbed my can-do little Goldstar for thirty bucks at a P.C. Richard & Son clearance sale (www.pcrichard.com). As long as you don't put certain things into it (aluminum foil, an egg, your cat), your projects will nearly always achieve doneness without mishap. The microwave cooks a few things well, but does an okay job with most things, and it does that job *fast*—which sometimes is really all you want or need. (My own feeling about microwaves is that any appliance that cooks a whole dinner during a single commercial break on *Law & Order* has a definite place in my kitchen.)

M any people who install eight-burner Viking ranges in their million-dollar kitchens ultimately find themselves using a toaster oven for just about everything they cook. And why the heck not? It's silly to bake a single pork chop in an oven big enough to roast a goat—and time-consuming too, since that large space can take a full 20 minutes to preheat. Putting the same chop in a snug little toaster oven featuring a glass door and an interior light, on the other hand, allows you to witness its magical transformation into dinner in a thrifty, up close and personal kind of way. At the same time this handy appliance taps into our many happy memories of that preferred toy of gourmand children everywhere, the Hasbro Easy-Bake oven (for a trip down memory lane, check it out: www.hasbro.com/easybake).

In the ultra-small kitchen and home, toaster ovens have the added benefits of (1) not heating up your place too much, (2) pre-heating almost instantly, (3) liberating you from the possibility of gas poisoning, and (4) freeing your regular oven (should you have one) for far more important small-apartment uses, such as storage of cookware, sweaters, and five-year-old tax returns.

If you are thinking of buying yourself a toaster oven, remember that the lowest-end toaster ovens can be dangerous and undependable; they can also be too small to cook anything larger than a frozen bagel. But high-end toaster ovens, often with convection or

microwave elements, can be countertop space hogs. So seek the
middle ground. The best features to look for in a toaster
oven include an interior light
(which not only lets you watch your

food cook in a way that is almost as entertaining as television but
also reminds you if you've unwittingly left the toaster oven on),
enough interior space (at least 5 inches from rack to roof, which is
enough to hold a $3^1/_2$-pound chicken), and an auto-shutoff device
(a safety and economy concern for all of us, not just the severely
absentminded). A removable crumb tray is nice, too. Some toaster
ovens are designed for under-cabinet or wall mounting, which can
help save space on your countertop, should you actually have some
under-cabinet space.

Incidentally, if you are trying to cook in a very primitive space
and lack so much as a stovetop, the Avanti Mini Kitchen, a compact
mini-oven and double hot plate combination (available through
Wal-Mart online for less than $100), may well be the answer to
your modest little prayers. A more elaborate model ($65 more) fea-
tures rotisserie and convection elements: view it online at
www.compactappliance.com.

Toaster ovens are fun, but hardly indispensable. If you have an
oven and broiler combination that functions well, you might prefer
using it, particularly if your counter space is limited and you are
concerned about the cost of electricity compared to gas (in some
rental homes, gas costs are included in the rent).

The best features to look for here include turntable, interior light and see-through window, variable and preprogrammed cook settings, moisture sensor, crisper pan, shortcut keys, and—last but not least—comprehensible instructions. Good luck.

And Also a Quick Word about Blenders

The best new blenders will now do the work of mixers and food processors—and in itty bitty kitchens, where limited counter space cuts down on the possibilities for countertop appliances, multi-taskers of this sort are *particularly* valuable. Nearly any blender will do for basic blending tasks (for ten years I managed very well with a used bar blender purchased for $5 at an Episcopal Church tag sale; I have no doubt it blended up many a daiquiri before it came into my life). But the most versatile combo-blender for small-kitchen cooking these days is surely the Cuisinart SmartPower™ Duet (approximately $80 at the Cuisinart Web site, www.cpokitchen.com, and elsewhere; not to be confused with its steroidal big brother, the SmartPower™ Premier Duet, which runs about $130). This miraculous and compact invention features a low, wide, and easily accessible 40-ounce glass jar as well as a 3-cup food processor work bowl that is really the perfect size for most home chopping and mixing jobs. Its Cuisinart motor will never jam or balk, and, oddly enough, its food processor element is simpler to operate than the grown-up version's, because it features a much less complicated safety mechanism.

Finally, the Floor

After your kitchen appliances have been scrubbed and adjusted to perfection, you'll need to finish your deep cleaning by swabbing the floor. Do it with gusto, since the sine qua non of a spotless kitchen is a floor "so clean you can eat off it." Wax it, too, if you can, to increase its shine and keep it dirt-resistant. Luckily your kitchen floor is tiny, so there's not much down there to swab—or to wax—or to eat.

———————

Now that your kitchen is spotless, you are probably brimming with excitement about all the adventures that await you in this marvelous new space. Enjoy these feelings while you can, because now we need to grapple with the biggest of all itty bitty problems: kitchen storage space.

3

*N*ow THAT YOU HAVE EMPTIED YOUR
KITCHEN SPACE OF STUFF, VETTED ALL ITS
APPLIANCES, AND DEEP CLEANED ITS EVERY INCH,
LET'S PAUSE TO RETHINK THE KITCHEN LAYOUT BEFORE STARTING TO
FILL THE PLACE BACK UP AGAIN. BECAUSE THAT'S ONE OF THE THINGS
ABOUT KITCHEN WORK: REPETITION. YOU ARE ALWAYS GOING THROUGH
CYCLES, RETURNING TO THE SAME THINGS OVER AND OVER AND OVER
AGAIN. EMPTY IT OUT, FILL IT BACK UP. USE IT UP, REPLENISH IT. TAKE IT
OUT, PUT IT AWAY. MAKE A MESS, CLEAN IT UP. SHOP, COOK, EAT, . . .
THEN SHOP, COOK, AND EAT AGAIN . . . AND AGAIN . . . AND *AGAIN*!

REPETITION IS ACTUALLY ONE OF THE MOST COMFORTING THINGS
ABOUT KITCHEN LIFE (CONSTANT LOVING ACTIVITY AND USE ARE, AFTER
ALL, WHAT MAKES A HOUSE A HOME), BUT REPETITION CAN ALSO BE

one of the most numbing and frustrating things about your kitchen work, particularly if you find yourself making the *same* awkward movements, caught in the *same* awkward situations, over and over and over again in that impossibly tiny little space you call home.

Here is where presence of mind, economy of motion, and a considered organization of kitchen items into a convenient, space-efficient storage system are all going to come in very, very handy. Good lighting will also be important, and so will design. So in this chapter we will focus on setting up the kitchen for ease of use, making sure everything is properly lit, ordered, and laid out. Once that's finished, we'll review some important facts about color, decoration, and lighting that can make small spaces seem not only bigger but also more welcoming, more safe, and more easy to use.

Clear the Decks: or, How Sailors Decorate

THE MOST SPACE-CHALLENGED KITCHENS IN THE WORLD are those aboard small sailboats, which is why nobody understands the mania for kitchen organization better than a small-sailboat galley slave. Growing up on a thirty-six-foot catamaran whose kitchen was essentially a camp stove, an ice chest, and a bucket, I learned early that a galley that can be packed away between mealtimes creates a space that then becomes available for any number of other good uses, such as napping, making ship-to-shore phone calls to girl-friends, or else just hiding out from the chore-dispensing captain. A "disappearing" kitchen will be equally crucial to you in your very small home if, as on a sailboat, your cooking area cannot be screened off or separated from your main living space. Organized correctly, this space will appear neutral, tidy, and visually pleasing; organized incorrectly and left unattended, it will make your entire home look like a flophouse in no time flat.

Most galleys on small boats consist of a single working counter-top, which along with the stove is the focal point of all food preparation. If your kitchen has only one countertop and that space is currently infringed upon by things that could go elsewhere, move them. Commit to keeping your one vital food preparation space cleared and ready for action, in a way that will also be visually pleasing (that is, visually neutral) between mealtimes.

Incidentally, you really do need at least *one* small countertop. If your kitchen is so small that you have no work space at all, create it with a sturdy board you place atop your sink; the board can be hung up on a wall or tucked away beside the refrigerator until needed. If your drawers are sturdy enough, you can fit a similar chopping board atop an opened drawer. If necessary, you can go outside your kitchen area and commandeer your dining table for food preparation. Alternatively, you might design a hinged counter-top that can fold open as needed. (It really all depends on what kind of space you are working with.)

Another important concern for anyone cooking on board a boat is secure footing. This is important in the landlubber's kitchen as well, since slipping on a wet or greasy floor is an occupational hazard for every busy cook, whether or not the floor happens to be rolling and pitching on a four-foot swell. If you spend a great deal of time standing in one place (and in a small kitchen it's a good bet that you will, since that's the only place *to* stand), your back is going to be much more prone to stress. The best way to alleviate that stress is by standing on a cushioning rubber mat. Professional kitchens rely on thick rubber grease mats to give their cooks secure and cushioned footing, but for the home cook, a thick rubber doormat can do an equally good job at a fraction of the price. If you don't like the look of rubber mats, consider utilizing a small, well-cushioned washable indoor-outdoor carpet mat with a nonstick rubber backing.

Because space management and secure stowage are so important to shipboard life, boat designers try to keep dish cupboards and cutlery drawers as close as possible to the galley sink. That way, dishes and utensils are secured immediately after washing. Your cutlery drawer and dish and glass storage should also be kept as close as possible to your sink, just to create economy of motion while washing dishes on dry land.

Boat galleys, like all IBKs, have minimal storage space, usually in awkward areas. Boat designers work hard to optimize whatever space is available, and so should you. If your lower cabinets are deep and hard to reach, for example, consider installing roll-out shelving to make the entire area readily accessible—because you are *much* more likely to cook if you can reach your pots and pans without risk of putting out your back. Lid storage, similarly, should be managed with racks that install inside cabinet doors, to keep all banging and clanking to a minimum.

Setting Up Particular Zones

ONCE YOU HAVE "IMPROVED" YOUR CABINETRY AND EDITED YOUR POSSESSIONS, you can begin to decide where the pots, pans, and dishes you need most go best. Feel free to be idiosyncratic. Only you know which items you reach for the most; and of course they should go in the closest and most convenient place possible, and change places as your cooking habits change.

If your space is extremely limited, consider creating an "annex" outside the kitchen for storage of least-used items. Even one extra shelf in a coat closet or one extra drawer in a bureau can free up your kitchen. Remember also that many things we habitually place in our kitchens do not really need to reside there. Vitamins can go into your medicine chest, cookbooks into bookcases. Cleaning supplies don't *all* need to reside in your under-sink cupboard; some can go in a broom closet or bathroom cabinet. Pet supplies can fit in those places, too. Bottles of wine can go in a provisional wine rack in your living room or else in a closet, as can liquor bottles. It's your home, so do what works for you.

Bottom line: If it's getting in the way of your cooking, it needs to move. You don't have to throw it away; just get it out of the kitchen.

Countertops

No countertop stays empty for long in the little kitchens of little homes, where any open horizontal space inevitably becomes a catchall for STUFF. If you are constantly leaving junk mail, telephone messages, credit card bills, memo pads, pens, house keys, mints, and nail clippers on your kitchen counter, set up a basket or tray for this kind of dumping, and make a point of toting it away and sorting through it elsewhere. Moving STUFF to another place in your small home will help break the psychological logjam that will otherwise keep you from your cooking.

Cupboards

If in doubt about how many dishes, bowls, cups, glasses, utensils, pots, and pans you will actually need, consult the suggestions in the next chapter, marvel at their simplicity, and return once again to the task of downsizing your possessions or putting them into out-of-kitchen storage. Your things should fit into cupboards *without crowding,* because the more crowded a space is, the more difficult it is to use.

Once you have done your final edit, consider a few inexpensive improvements to your cabinets. If the cabinets do not extend all the way up to the ceiling, purchase washable containers that will fit into that unused space. Cardboard containers are no good here, and neither is open storage, since the upper areas of any kitchen are exposed to large amounts of vaporized kitchen grease and sticky dust.

Next, look at your options for organizing the insides of your cabinets. Pull-out pantry systems can install in spaces as small as a broom closet; adjustable spice racks specifically designed to be mounted on the inside of a cabinet door can organize your herbs and spices for easiest access without exposing them to heat or light; lazy Susans (including corner-mounting and pull-out varieties) will keep your canned goods visible and accessible. Consider installing full-extension basket pullouts for low cabinets and even under-sink cabinets (which can be fitted with special shelving that installs around existing plumbing). Remember that adding an extra shelf or two to dish cabinets can make plates more easily accessible. All of these accessories can be placed into existing cabinetry at minimal expense; buy them very economically from Closetmaid, www.closetmaid.com, or else through The Container Store, www.containerstore.com. These manufacturers also make tray dividers, slide-out and tilt-out bins, easy-access garbage bag holders, and plate stackers. They make gadgets for items that do not stack well, too. Cups, for example, can be suspended from a series of hooks mounted on a rod that pulls out for easy access; wineglasses can be organized by installing a preassembled stemware rack to the bottom of an existing cabinet or under a shelf within that cabinet.

Only you know the needs and dimensions of your particular cabinets, and only you can decide how much time and money you want to spend making that space optimally efficient. To survey the fittings that can help you improve your storage ability, take a look at one of the best inexpensive sources of cabinet fittings, the elfa storage system, particularly its mini-kitchen line, available at The Container Store or online at www.organize-everything.com. Ikea has its own ranges of cabinet fittings that install easily into any cupboard. The many ingenious storage solutions available there can be browsed quickly online at www.ikea-usa.com.

You don't necessarily need to spend money in order to organize. You can improvise a storage system for baking sheets, cutting boards, and trays, for example, by simply using a vertical file holder. All you *really* need to get organized is the desire to do so, and the energy (and focus) to follow through.

Nice Drawers!

If in doubt about how much cutlery and how many utensils you need, consult the suggestions on pages 56–58. A brief glance at this orderly and limited assortment should be enough to convince

 you that your own drawers, with their current jumble of tools, flatware, disposable chopsticks, broken eyeglasses, pens, fast-food menus, matchbooks, mints, dental floss, Chap Stick, and five-year-old dog heartworm medicine, need some serious editing down.

Once you have reduced your cutlery and kitchen utensils to the essentials, you may well find that all of these items can fit in a single drawer. New expandable drawer organizers (www.organizes-it.com and elsewhere) can banish the "dead space" between conventional drawer organizers and your drawer walls—and while nobody else is now

going to mistake your kitchen drawers for Martha's drawers at
Turkey Hill Farm, you will certainly notice a satisfying improvement.

For Those Who Must Have More

If your kitchen drawers have no available room for your utensils, or
if you are extremely fond of extra utensils, consider the following
options:

Sneak one in. Fit extra shallow drawers into your existing under-
counter cabinets, using either the elfa or Ikea systems. You'll need to
open a cabinet to get at these secondary drawers, but they'll still be
right there in your kitchen.

Tool time. Try keeping your utensils in a toolbox that you break out
at cooking time. This high-testosterone look is particularly appropriate for those who enjoy using a Dremel drill to bore holes in their
Christmas cookies or fire up a butane torch at the mention of crème
brûlée.

Trucker's dream. If you are truly gadget crazy, consider the Sears
Craftsman Eight-Drawer Roll Away, the wheeled tool bench of
choice for garage mechanics everywhere (approximately $250;
www.sears.com; Sears item #00965802000; Mfr. model #65802). Its
shallow drawers are specifically designed to hold every conceivable
sort of tool (including kitchen tools) in a single layer; it will also

hold wraps, cutlery, utensils, spices, and just about anything else you'd care to put into it. Throw a butcher-block top on this wheeled wonder and it becomes a sensationally efficient kitchen island, storage chest, minibar, and conversation piece. (If you're not big on a "Chop Shop" aesthetic, consider other wheeled kitchen carts that can reside outside the kitchen—such as any of the numerous models available through www.organizes-it.com.)

"Junk" drawer rehab. **An** easier strategy, of course, would be simply to banish your kitchen "junk" drawer and reclaim the space in the name of bona fide kitchen items. Since many drawers are soon cluttered up with plastic wrap, tinfoil, and paper towels, consider mounting a combined foil, plastic wrap, and paper towel dispenser on a wall. You'll want a contemporary dispenser that is neutral in color and design, has very good ability to cut, and accepts the size of paper towel roll you use. The Frieling Triple Roll Dispenser, available online for approximately $20 at www.frieling.com, has the added benefit of releasing the top (plastic wrap) compartment for handheld use.

About That Sink Setup

One of the great shocks of small-kitchen living to the present generation is: no dishwasher. In the move to a small, one- or two-person apartment, some of us are facing life without this miracle of domestic technology for the very first time. As a result, we have to brace ourselves (and set up our sinks) for honest-to-goodness dishwashing.

A full description of dishwashing awaits in Chapter 8, along with instructions for dishwashing newbies and a couple of tantalizing possibilities for small-space automatic dishwashing. Important sink accessories are listed there as well, so flip ahead to pages 206–207 and add them to your shopping list.

Arrangement and Storage of Pantry Items

As you return your food staples to your newly cleaned and newly improved cupboards, consider these guidelines in choosing how and where to place your food.

Proper temperature and light. Cupboards above stovetops, toaster ovens, and refrigerators are too warm generally to store perishables (spices, oils, canned fish, wine, coffee, bread, cookies, and biscuits). If slightly too-warm storage is all that's available, you'll have to store more of your things in the refrigerator, or else store fewer things overall, buying the more perishable items only as needed.

Group like things accordingly. In order to keep food items from getting lost or going AWOL (think of those five-year-old marshmallow

Peeps that suddenly emerge from the depths of your spice cabinet like so many bright yellow Rip Van Winkles), sort and consolidate foods according to type. That way you'll always know what you have and where to find it.

Arrange it in a cook-friendly way. **Try** consolidating all your food into one cupboard or area so that you know what you have at a glance, and keep that list of your staple items handy—preferably in a clear plastic sleeve on the cupboard's inside shelf. In elevated cabinets holding many small items, consider buying stepped shelving for visibility all the way to the back. (Incidentally, you can make your own stepped shelving by cutting 2 × 4 lumber to fit, stacking it as needed.) If you are a short person (or your cabinets are up high), consider buying yourself a foldaway step stool so that you have access to every last inch of IBK space.

Inspect. **Cull** and condense food items at least once a month. Make sure packages are sealed. Keep on the lookout for spoilage, aging, and pantry pests. If you are moving and had trouble with bugs in your previous residence, discard all foods in which bugs or their progeny might lurk.

Dare to discard. **If** you purchased an item a while ago, ask yourself if you ever really intend to use it, or if you're simply postponing the decision to throw it out. A canned good with no prospect of consumption can linger in your cupboard for years unless you take decisive action. (How old is that creamed corn?)

Rubbish!

One of the greatest ordeals you will face while working in your IBK is managing your trash. There are two schools of thought here. The first is to hide the garbage in a cabinet, usually under the sink. But in adopting this seemingly elegant solution, you not only give away precious under-counter storage but also create an environment in which forgotten waste becomes an all-you-can-eat buffet for legions of darkness-loving cockroaches—as well as a permanent source of lingering, hard-to-eradicate trash odor that no amount of air freshener will ever be able to tame.

Your less visually attractive option is to keep the garbage out in plain sight. A lidded trash can, though inevitably underfoot, is at least securely pest-proof, and the very fact of its visibility means it never goes untended. A compact, tightly lidded receptacle is best for small kitchens, whether or not you choose to hide your trash in a cabinet; line it with plastic garbage bags sized specifically for the container, empty it often, and wash out the plastic lining regularly, rinsing with a solution of 4 tablespoons baking soda per quart of water to complete the deodorization process.

If your garbage must be stored in an awkward or hard-to-reach place, try keeping a small plastic bucket or bowl on your counter-top for food scraps and waste. Use it during meal preparation, then empty and wash it out during cleanup time. Doing so will save you lots of twisting and stooping, which is a particularly difficult maneuver if you cook in a tight space.

As for recycling: Try to get all recyclables out of your kitchen as soon as possible. Rinse all recyclable glass, plastic, and aluminum containers, and take them out, however few there may be, along with each batch of trash.

Pets in the IBK pose a particular challenge to the space-deprived cook, particularly since our little friends usually crowd in on us just when we need personal space most. Yet we can hardly blame them for getting underfoot just as we engage in the most interesting household activity of the day—handling food that may, after all, find its way down to them!

If you need to exclude your pet from the kitchen during mealtimes, consider keeping a child safety gate at the entrance—thus keeping your pet (and other potential interlopers) out. Barricading yourself into your own little kitchen with a device designed for toddlers may initially seem absurd, but it's better than constantly stepping on or over your pet as you attempt to drain off a pot of boiling pasta water or hack the spine out of a chicken.

One strategy for coexisting with pets and their dishes is to feed your animal first, then lift its dish (and clean it!) before starting your own cooking. That way, your pet's food dish will always be spotless, and you, meanwhile, will have one less thing to trip over as you cook or clean for yourself. (Also please note that a full-bellied pet is much less likely to solicit handouts.) If you are feeling particularly stressed, crowded, or claustrophobic, you might alternatively consider temporarily placing your pet's food and water bowls in your entry hall or bathroom—and, if necessary, your pet along with them.

Coping with Real-Life Kitchen Claustrophobia

IT'S ALL VERY WELL TO JOKE about having a kitchen so small that it brings on a panic attack—but what if it really does?

Claustrophobia—a persistent, abnormal, and irrational fear of confined or small spaces—is, like all phobias, a condition to which some people are genetically predisposed, but which is almost always rooted in some traumatic past experience. Symptoms of a claustrophobic panic attack typically include shortness of breath, dizziness, nausea, chills, sweating, rapid breathing, irregular heartbeat, weakness in the knees, and hot flashes—as well as overall feelings of dread, terror, and fear of going crazy or dying.

Claustrophobic panic attacks are usually

stress-related, and are initially triggered by something that has led our subconscious mind to link being in that confined space with some past emotional trauma. But the fear of physical restriction is quite natural, and hardly unique to humans; in many wild animals—birds and dolphins, for example—the reaction can be so powerful that it causes stress-induced sudden death.

Luckily, our species can overcome its tendency to panic. If you suffer from small-kitchen claustrophobia, you might search back into your past for the small-space experience that first caused such feelings. You might also consider that your panic response is not triggered so much by the small size of the room as by the fact that the room is a kitchen—for not all kitchens are as happy as the cozy little one over which you currently preside.

If you can't control small-kitchen freakouts, what are your options? Self-medicating is hardly practical: popping a Xanax every time you need to chop an onion is really not the answer. Instead, consider working with a therapist to recognize and understand the past trauma that is causing your panic response. Once you have done so, you can begin to connect positive feelings to your small kitchen space rather than the negative ones that now dominate your subconscious mind. Outside of therapy you can continue the process by improving your kitchen space physically, so that it feels like a safe, friendly, pleasant place in which you actually *choose* to work. Your comfort level will increase if you regularly spend time in your kitchen and have more and more good experiences there. As your unconscious realizes that you are safe and happy in your IBK, your claustrophobic panic will vanish—with luck, forever.

Super-cleanliness and complete organization will also play a big part in keeping you happy and calm.

Design Strategies for Kitchen Claustrophobics

WHEN SETTING UP YOUR SMALL KITCHEN, you don't want to make that little space any more panic-inducing than it already is. By carefully selecting lighting, paints, floors, and mirrors, and also by minimizing clutter, you may not be able to change the size of your kitchen, but you *will* be able to change your subconscious perception of its size, which can make an enormous difference in your comfort level. Let's look at each strategy.

Lighting

Good clear lighting is necessary to cooking and cleaning, and moreover a well-lit space appears larger. Most kitchens feature strong overhead lighting, either incandescent or fluorescent. But fluorescent light will cast a sickly, bluish glow on people and food alike, creating glare that can cause headaches, tension, and stress and turn your kitchen into a food morgue.

One way to bring your *Dawn of the Dead* kitchen back to the land of the living is to purchase a fluorescent bulb that has been color-adjusted to simulate natural light. Known as full-spectrum or daylight fluorescent bulbs, these little wonders are available either as compact fluorescent or linear fluorescent bulbs, with wattages anywhere from 11 to 42 watts. Another very easy way to improve the quality of your fluorescent lighting (though it should really go without saying!) is to clean the light fixture in which it resides—in your minimally ventilated kitchen area this fixture will quickly become greasy, dusty, and filthy if left unattended. Finally and most effectively, you can add extra (incandescent) lighting to supplement that main fluorescent fixture.

Overhead incandescent lighting can be improved similarly, with full-spectrum bulbs adjusted to simulate daylight: both GE and Sylvania produce them (and again, clean your fixtures). A dimmer switch can help you to adjust light levels during those moments when full-bore overhead lighting is just too harsh for comfort; a dimmer is particularly useful if your kitchen is part of your main living space. Since full-spectrum light from both fluorescent and incandescent sources is thought to ameliorate SAD (Seasonal Affective Disorder, the depression that comes with wintertime light deprivation), if you are at all depressive (and who isn't?), definitely give these lightbulbs a try.

If you want to increase area lighting without invading counter space, consider under-cabinet lighting; with a dimmer switch added, a simple incandescent utility light mounted under a cabinet can create a variety of moods, from clinical to cozy to sacral. A row of ceiling-mounted downlights (that is, lighting that directs a beam of light downward, either at an angle or vertically) can perform similar transformations. Even a simple night-light plugged into a wall socket is often all a dark kitchen corner needs to boost work light (and cheeriness) to acceptable levels.

Finally, if you have deep, dark under-counter cabinets, consider mounting inexpensive battery-operated lights inside that you can turn on and off as needed.

You don't need to hire an electrician to make improvements to your kitchen lighting: Downlighting, under-counter light fixtures, and incandescent lamps can all be bought inexpensively and installed even by those of us who have minimal tool-handling skills. Outfits like Ikea and Home Depot will help you with any specific questions you might have about doing so, and in some cases will even perform installations on your behalf.

Paint, Wall Colors, and Wall Treatments

Light, bright walls and cabinets, preferably painted white, are more reflective and will maximize the effects of both natural and artificial lighting in a small space. Because your kitchen needs to be repainted more often than the rest of your home, sophisticated wall treatments and custom paint jobs are hardly recommended here, but if you do decide to go with a patterned wallpaper or stencil, make sure the design is small and discreet, and that your wallpaper is tough and washable.

Whatever wall treatment you choose, remember to leave your ceilings white to maximize brightness. Also, keep in mind that when cabinets and walls are the same color, they are less confusing to the eye and thereby create an impression of greater space—and, again, white cabinets are best for improving a sense of spaciousness. If your cabinets are exceptionally ugly, remember that old or unattractive cabinet doors can usually be resurfaced without removing the entire cabinet, and that doing so is much more economical. Even

refrigerator DOOR clutter

In really small kitchens and homes, the refrigerator door is often a message center and magnetic catchall for everything from dry cleaning slips to discount coupons to yoga schedules. While it's good to keep a memo pad, a few magnets, and the occasional piece of child art on your refrigerator, much of the STUFF that ends up there doesn't really need to be there. If you move it elsewhere, your kitchen will look much less cluttered (and much more organized).

replacing cabinet handles, a tiny job, can make a noticeable difference to your space.

Mirrors

To increase the sense of space in your kitchen and improve light quality as well, install built-in mirrors in the area between your countertops and cabinets. Mirrors wipe clean easily and never absorb grease; so long as you aren't in the habit of throwing dishes or punches, they will last as long as your kitchen. Mirrors will probably also appeal to your vanity and your desire for company—particularly the sort that will never criticize, second-guess, or bump into you while you cook.

But beware: Like all mirrors, kitchen mirrors need to be cleaned on a weekly basis to stay sparkling, and mirrors behind stovetops and sinks will particularly need your attention. Mirrors will also double the apparent clutter on your countertops, so if you're going to install mirrors, make sure that you're a clean-countertop type, or be ready to (literally) face the consequences.

Hanging Items

Many kitchens are decorated with overhead racks for hanging pots and pans. Attempt the same sort of overhead arrangement in a tiny kitchen, however, and you quickly create a clanking, dripping *Das Boot* effect that only increases the claustrophobic nature of the space. Hung objects (and open shelving) are also dust catchers and grease magnets in small, busy, minimally ventilated IBKs. If you are interested in hanging items on your walls—which can be a very useful way of storing frequently used cooking utensils—install an inexpensive wire wall grid (available at www.organize-everything.com in dimensions of 18 × 24 inches or 24 × 36 inches) or Peg-Board (available at your hardware store, cut to measure), proceed with caution, and desist as and when claustrophobia strikes.

One way to hang an item without banging an actual hole in your wall or investing in an entire mounting rack is by using removable hooks. 3M's Command line of mounting products (www.3m.com/us/home_leisure/command) offers you a hook system using a special adhesive that can be attached and detached from walls with no surface damage whatsoever. Inexpensive hooks that attach via suction cup, meanwhile, work beautifully on any smooth surface, including mirrors, glass, enameled sinks, cabinets, refrigerators, and stoves. Attach both types of hooks to suit any passing whim, knowing you can remove them at any time.

Wall-Mounted and Built-in Appliances

Your very small kitchen has little free counter space for appliances, even the ones you use most. If at all possible, mount these appliances in or under existing cabinetry. Many toasters, toaster ovens, coffeemakers, and microwaves are nowadays designed specifically for such installation (as indeed are radios, small television sets, and DVD players, all of which can be nice to have around if you spend lots of time cooking and cleaning). Remember, though, that toasters and toaster ovens are going to throw off a good deal of heat, so cabinets above them ought not be ones holding perishable food.

Open Headroom

Open kitchen storage is more difficult to maintain than cabinet storage in an IBK (because of the concentration of vaporized grease and dust), but it is often more beautiful to look at, and if you really are suffering from claustrophobia in your kitchen, removing a cabinet or two to create a more open feeling at head level may well be your answer. You give away storage space, but you gain light and air. Your new open shelves will require you to be more tidy and neat, but then again, if you're naturally tidy, like keeping things on display, and don't mind doing a little extra cleaning, this is definitely the way to go.

Last, a Personal Touch

While the itty bitty kitchen is not a space that lends itself to opulent decor, you can still express yourself there. Something as simple as a fresh flower in a vase, an odd little toy, or a crayon drawing by a favorite nephew can make all the difference to your feelings about that (formerly) scary little space. Remember: No IBK is complete until you are totally happy and at home in it.

4

*S*tocking A SMALL KITCHEN WITH COOK

WARE SHOULD BE A SIMPLE BUSINESS, BUT IT ISN'T.

WHY? BECAUSE MOST POT, PAN, BAKEWARE, DISH-

WARE, AND FLATWARE SETS ARE PUT TOGETHER FOR A REGULAR-SIZED

KITCHEN AND THE STORAGE AREA THAT COMES WITH IT—THAT IS, THE

KITCHEN OF A LARGER HOME, IN WHICH MEALS FOR FOUR TO SIX PEO-

PLE ARE ROUTINELY BEING PREPARED. BUT IF YOU WERE TO BRING THESE

HIGHLY ECONOMICAL BOXED SETS INTO YOUR ITTY BITTY KITCHEN,

THERE WOULD PROBABLY BE VERY LITTLE ROOM LEFT FOR YOU, YOUR

FOOD, OR YOUR COOKING! SO YOU MUST INSTEAD ACQUIRE ALL YOUR

PIECES À LA CARTE, OR ELSE BUY A WHOLE SET AND GIVE HALF AWAY, OR

ELSE (MOST LIKELY SCENARIO) KEEP THE WHOLE SET AND ONCE AGAIN

PLUG UP YOUR KITCHEN WITH **STUFF**.

But just as one perfectly tailored suit is better than five cheap suits that fit badly, a small amount of cookware that suits your needs perfectly is always going to be better than a large amount of mediocre, space-hogging sᴛᴜꜰꜰ. So don't rush into the purchase of boxed sets. Take your time acquiring new pieces until you know exactly what you want—and before buying anything large or expensive, try out similar things by picking them up at yard sales and thrift shops (or else by borrowing them from friends) just to see if these tantalizing objects really are as useful or worthwhile as they seem. (If not, discard or return them.) Finally, feel free to mix and match pots, pans, and dishes to suit your own specific cooking, serving, and eating habits. For encouragement in this eclectic yet discriminating approach to stocking a kitchen, take a look at the unmatched (in both senses of the word) cookware in Julia Child's now legendary kitchen, preserved for all eternity at the Smithsonian Institution and on its Web site: http://americanhistory.si.edu/juliachild/default.asp.

(Can) Opening Remarks

IN THIS CHAPTER, we are going to look at the basic contents of an itty bitty kitchen. Because each kitchen and cook are different, however, adjust each group of suggested items to your own particular tastes, needs, and (especially) storage requirements; in other words, make your own decisions based on your own habits and space.

In the event that you already have more kitchen equipment than you need, use these groups as a way of eliminating extra STUFF: If it's not among the suggested items on this list, consider taking it out of your kitchen, at least temporarily, and seeing if you miss it.

If your kitchen is already in fighting trim, you are probably going to find this chapter *monumentally* boring—so just skip on ahead to the next.

First, Your Tableware

Stop for a moment and figure out the maximum number of people you will ever want to cook for in your itty bitty home. (In my own home that number is four, because I can't seat more than four at my table.) Now remember that, if you ever *were* to serve a larger meal, you could always use disposable tableware—given the size of your digs, no one would ever hold it against you.

If you are truly space-limited and guest-phobic, you can reduce the four settings to two. If, on the other hand, you currently have more than four settings, don't discard the extras; just move them out of the kitchen so that you'll have room there for the things you really do need, and room enough to operate.

Glassware: Clink!

Stock your glasses according to your drinking and entertaining preferences, again in limited quantities. Because your few glasses are going to be in almost constant use, selecting the strongest and heaviest possible glasses makes the best sense. German and Czech makers of rugged lead-free crystal such as Stoelzle-oberglas offer top-quality glassware in an economical price range—approximately $2.50 to $3.50 per glass—and these crystal glasses make a really great clinking sound when you toast. You can also buy these glasses individually, so they're easily replaced. (Find them at Foster's Urban Homewares, on the net at www.Shopfosters.com.) Remember that not only are cheaper glasses much less clinkalicious; they also break much more easily—so they are really no great bargain.

Flatware

If you want to ditch that grungy college stuff and buy some excellent new flatware (a matched set is *awfully* civilized), keep in mind that most department stores sell complete settings in sets of four as well as the more usual bunches of eight to twelve. Keep the name and maker of your flatware pattern in your kitchen files in case you want to double or triple your holdings when/if you move to a larger place.

If, on the other hand, you already have a set for more than four, remove the extras from your kitchen area and place them in storage. Remember: The fewer pieces you have, the fewer pieces will pile up unwashed in your sink.

Utensils

Here's the fun stuff. Not many of these items are expensive, but if you have exceptionally limited resources, look for them at yard sales and thrift shops—where even top-quality, like-new kitchen items can usually be picked up for pennies on the dollar.

1   SMALL FINE-MESH SIEVE

1   STURDY MEDIUM SIEVE

1   GOOD-QUALITY ADJUSTABLE-GRIND PEPPER MILL

1   SALTSHAKER (AND, OPTIONALLY, A SMALL BOWL FOR SEA SALT AND OTHER COARSE-GRAINED SALTS, WHICH WILL NOT POUR THROUGH A SHAKER)

1   HARDWOOD MIXING SPOON

1   STURDY (NON-BENDY) LARGE-BOWLED NONSTICK COOKING SPOON

1   SET OF MEASURING SPOONS*

1   PINT-SIZED GLASS LIQUID MEASURING CUP*

1   SET OF NESTING DRY MEASURING CUPS

3   NESTING GLASS MIXING BOWLS WITH MATCHING RUBBERIZED LIDS*

1   VEGETABLE PEELER

1   MANUAL KNIFE SHARPENER

1   BASIC MANDOLINE WITH HAND GUARD (LEIFHEIT 4 IN 1 GRATER, A BRILLIANT DEVICE, IS AVAILABLE FOR $16.99 AT WWW.FINECOOKWARE.COM; THE BENRINER, WHICH HAS AN ADJUSTABLE BLADE AND A CULTLIKE FOLLOWING, IS $39.95 AT WWW.AMAZON.COM; THE OXO GOOD GRIPS MANDOLINE, FLAWLESSLY DESIGNED, IS $69.99 AT WWW.OXO.COM— EXPENSIVE, BUT EVERY COOK'S FANTASY)

1   MICROPLANE COARSE WIDE GRATER (AT WWW.BEDBATHANDBEYOND.COM AND ELSEWHERE FOR $14.99)

1   KITCHEN TIMER (PREFERABLY MAGNETIZED, FOR SPACE-SAVING PLACEMENT ON YOUR REFRIGERATOR; SKIP THIS ITEM IF YOU HAVE A MICROWAVE OR STOVE WITH A BUILT-IN TIMER)

1   CAN OPENER

*These are best purchased as part of the Pyrex 15-piece New Beginnings Set ($40 at www.Macys.com).

1	CHURCH KEY OPENER FOR BOTTLES AND CANS
1	STURDY NONSTICK POTATO MASHER
1	NONSTICK PIE SERVER
1	NONSTICK 9-INCH LOCKING TONGS
1	BASIC INSTANT-READ MEAT THERMOMETER (TRUTEMP INSTANT READ DIGITAL THERMOMETER FOR $9.99 AT WWW.TARGET.COM)
2	HEAT-RESISTANT RUBBER SPATULAS: SPOON SPATULA, FLAT SPATULA
1	CONVENTIONAL (FLAT) NONSTICK SPATULA (THAT IS, A PANCAKE TURNER)
1	NONSTICK FLAT WHISK
1	VEGETABLE STEAMER BASKET INSERT
3	PLASTIC CHOPPING BOARDS, SIZED LARGE, MEDIUM, AND SMALL—THE LARGEST HAVING A GROOVED EDGE TO CATCH MEAT JUICES AND THE MEDIUM IN A DIFFERENT COLOR, TO BE USED EXCLUSIVELY FOR PREPARING RAW FISH, MEAT, AND POULTRY, IN ORDER TO AVOID CROSS-CONTAMINATION
1	SMALL GLASS JAR (AN EMPTY MUSTARD JAR) FOR SALAD DRESSING
1	TRAY LARGE ENOUGH TO HOLD A COMPLETE MEAL
1	TRIVET
4	COTTON OR LINEN DISH TOWELS
2	POT HOLDERS
4	COTTON NAPKINS

OPTIONAL:
1	LADLE
1	SMALL BAKING/COOLING RACK
1	ELECTRIC FOOD-WARMING TRAY (ONLY IF YOU LIKE TO ENTERTAIN)

Pots and Pans

1   COFFEEPOT (OR COFFEE MACHINE) OF CHOICE

1   NONSTICK MEDIUM SAUCEPAN, APPROXIMATELY 1 QUART, PREFERABLY
     WITH A LOCK-ON, SELF-STRAINING LID (CIRCULON, $19.95,
     WWW.MACY'S.COM)

1   3$^{1}/_{2}$-QUART ENAMELED CAST-IRON DUTCH OVEN WITH LID

1   NONSTICK OMELET PAN WITH LID TO COVER (WHICH WILL NEED TO BE
     BOUGHT OR FOUND SEPARATELY, BECAUSE OMELET PANS DON'T COME
     WITH LIDS)

1   (STICK OR NONSTICK) LIDDED SAUTÉ PAN

1   SMALL NONSTICK SAUCEPAN, HOLDING APPROXIMATELY 2 TO 3 CUPS
     (OFTEN DESCRIBED AS A BUTTER WARMER)

1   NONSTICK 3-QUART SAUCIER, PREFERABLY WITH A LOCK-ON, SELF-
     STRAINING LID (CIRCULON, $39.95, WWW.SEARS.COM)

OPTIONAL: 1   SPATTER SCREEN (PACKS FLAT, COSTS APPROXIMATELY $3)

           1   TEAKETTLE

Once again, *your pots need not match.*

If you are inclined to bring your pots to the table or leave them in plain sight between mealtimes because you have no storage space, it's better to have handsome pots than ugly ones, so stainless steel, which stays clean and shiny—unlike aluminum (which dulls), copper (which tarnishes), and iron (which needs special care)—might be the way to go, at least for some items. Then again stainless-steel pots are simply too heavy for many folks, particularly when stacked inside one another in low cabinets. So if you have lower back issues,

With just a little ingenuity you can use the basic equipment in your kitchen to substitute for many specialized appliances and gadgets that will otherwise take up lots of room:

Salad spinner: Wash greens in the sink, then shake them dry and gently remove any remaining water on salad greens with a clean kitchen towel. Store the greens in the same towel until serving time.

Freestanding colander: Replace with a self-straining saucepan or handled sieve.

Big pasta pot: Cook your pasta in less water, using at most a 3-quart saucepan (see "Itty Bitty Pasta: Shortcut Central," page 128).

Coffee machine: Reclaim lost counter space by using a *stovetop* coffee pot (aha!), or a stowable filter-and-thermos jug combination, or a Melitta plastic filter cone for one cup.

Espresso machine: A small and inexpensive aluminum stovetop Moka espresso pot, available at most hardware stores for approximately $20, can help you reclaim valuable countertop space and at the same time save you bucks on all those $3.59 store-bought lattes. (To make foamy milk for cappuccino, heat your milk in a nonstick saucepan and whip it with a whisk, an immersion blender, or an eggbeater.)

Funnel and/or pastry bag: Cut the corner off a plastic storage bag; dispose of it after use.

Toasted sandwich maker: A weighted pot lid pressed down on a sandwich that is being gently toasted in a nonstick skillet can approximate the work of a panini press. (You can also use a teakettle filled with hot water as the weight.)

Crock-Pot: Just use a lidded nonstick ovenproof pot set in a very low oven. The low setting on a Crock-Pot is 200 degrees F, the high setting, 300 degrees F.

Food processor: An inexpensive mandoline (such as the Leifheit 4 in 1 Grater, page 57) can handle most food-processing slicing jobs—and, hey, it packs flat! A blender, an immersion blender, a combination blender, a whisk, or a stowable lightweight handheld mixer will take care of most other food processor needs (except bread dough, which was kneaded by hand for several thousand years before the advent of the Cuisinart).

weak wrists, or awkward, limited pot storage that is going to require a lot of stacking and stooping, nonstick aluminum may well be for you. If you're conflicted, why not some of both?

The same applies to the question of nonstick or regular cookware. Most people agree that a regular (stainless steel) sauté pan can create deeper, richer sauces. If you like to make sauces, it might be worth your while to have one.

Oven and Bakeware

These smaller dishes are particularly useful in an IBK. They can do double duty serving anything from cocktail nibbles to puddings, so don't think of them as extravagances.

FOUR 8-OUNCE RAMEKINS

FOUR 4-OUNCE RAMEKINS

2 SINGLE-SERVING-SIZE GRATIN DISHES

9-INCH OR 9^{1}/$_{2}$-INCH OVENPROOF GLASS PIE DISH WITH RUBBERIZED LID*

8 × 8-INCH BAKING DISH WITH RUBBERIZED LID*

9 × 9-INCH BAKING DISH

If you are lucky enough to have a real oven, you might also add

ONE 9 × 13-INCH OVENPROOF BAKING DISH WITH RUBBERIZED LID*

1 HEAVY-GAUGE JELLY-ROLL PAN/COOKIE SHEET

1 MEDIUM (APPROXIMATELY 3^{1}/$_{2}$ QUARTS) LIDDED CASSEROLE

*See note on Pyrex set (page 57).

Food Storage Ware

Nobody ever seems to notice that commercially produced plastic storage ware sets are *themselves* a storage problem: The many shapes and sizes, which never quite nest up, can take over an entire cabinet when not in use.

By limiting the types of storage ware in your kitchen to a maximum of three inter-stacking varieties, you can create a compact storage arsenal. Remember that items that will not fit the largest of these containers can be stored in your glass mixing bowls and baking dishes with their matching rubberized lids, or else in your lidded casserole or Dutch oven, or else simply in zipper-locking plastic bags or plastic wrap.

The new disposable storage ware (from Gladware and Ziploc) is widely available and relatively cheap—so cheap that you will not shrink from fast, no-guilt, no-mess purging of really funky leftovers that you can't bear to open up and wash out. (If you go for these disposable wares, though, be warned: You will need to choose one brand or the other, since Gladware is mostly square or rectangular, while Ziploc is primarily round.) An even more cunning alternative is the stackable Smart Spin storage system that holds twenty-four containers (24, 16, and 8 ounces) and twenty-four entirely interchangeable lids on a patented retractable lazy Susan that takes up less than one square foot of space. (Available for $19.99 at www.asseenontvnetwork.com or 1-800-626-1300.) But you can approximate the same system by simply engaging in the tried-and-true bachelor trick of saving the lidded safety-lock plastic containers from Chinese take-out soups and deli items—or else by purchasing these very same containers new (!) from their *actual* manufacturer at www.usplastic.com. They cost 35 to 55 cents apiece (with lid) depending on size; can be reused indefinitely; are safe for refrigerator, freezer, and microwave; and are inexpensive enough that you can ditch them without the slightest twinge of remorse.

4 CYLINDRICAL 8-OUNCE CONTAINERS WITH LIDS

4 CYLINDRICAL 16-OUNCE CONTAINERS WITH LIDS

4 CYLINDRICAL 32-OUNCE CONTAINERS WITH LIDS

And then, of course, there are assorted wraps and bags, which can also claim a good deal of drawer space unless placed in their own holder mounted inside a cabinet door (available at Lowes or Home Depot). A low-cost alternative for organizing wraps is the cardboard six-pack container designed for bottles of beer or soft drinks: Remove the bottles, and insert a box of wrap in each empty space. Following are some suggested wraps:

1 ROLL OF ALUMINUM FOIL, PREFERABLY NONSTICK

1 ROLL OF PLASTIC WRAP, EITHER PRESS AND SEAL OR REGULAR

1 ROLL OF WAX PAPER OR FREEZER PAPER

3 BOXES OF STORAGE BAGS WITH "LOCKING" AIRTIGHT CLOSURE IN THE FOLLOWING SIZES: 1 QUART, 1 GALLON, AND SANDWICH-SIZED

Kitchen Knives

Although large sets of knives are often for sale at bargain prices, Julia Child has long since decreed (to unanimous agreement from chefs the world over) that a good chef's knife, paring knife, and serrated knife are all any home cook really ever needs. This is good news for anyone with an itty bitty kitchen, since knife storage can take up so much precious countertop, wall, and drawer space. The important thing about your three knives is, they must be *very good knives* and must be kept in *very good condition*—which means washing and drying them promptly after use, storing them in protective sleeves (either commercially available plastic "knife safe blade protectors"— $3.99 at www.organizes-it.com—or your own, homemade cardboard sheaths), giving them a sharpening whenever they dull, and never, *ever* using them to cut through empty beer cans as seen on the legendary Ginsu knife commercial.

Good knives need not cost a fortune. The highest-rated chef's knife in a recent survey by *Cook's Illustrated* magazine cost less than $30: the Forschner 8-inch Chef's Knife (fibrox handle). It can be found easily online (www.premiumknives.com; 1-877-541-4076). A good paring knife can likewise be bought for less than $10.

———————————

That's it— you're all set. Now on to Part 2 of this little manual, in which we talk about the things you will actually *do* in your newly organized IBK: cooking, cleaning, and, yes, entertaining.

PART 2

FUN IN THE ITTY BITTY KITCHEN

5

First the Good News

There ARE SOME WONDERFUL ADVANTAGES TO SMALL-SPACE AND SMALL-QUANTITY COOKING, SO BEFORE PLUNGING INTO THE MANY BRILLIANT STRATEGIES NEEDED FOR PLAYING A STRONG OFFENSIVE GAME IN YOUR IBK, LET'S PAUSE FIRST AND KNEEL TO COUNT OUR ITTY BITTY BLESSINGS.

FIRST BLESSING: BECAUSE YOU ARE (PROBABLY) GOING TO COOK FOR JUST ONE OR TWO OTHER PEOPLE IN YOUR LITTLE HOME, YOU ARE GOING TO BE WORKING WITH MUCH SMALLER QUANTITIES OF FOOD THAN MOST PEOPLE. THIS KIND OF COOKING IS GREAT BECAUSE IT INVOLVES SO MUCH LESS PREP WORK.

SECOND BLESSING: YOU ARE NOW GOING TO BE ABLE TO EXPERIMENT WITH NEW FOODS AND NEW RECIPES, INDULGING YOURSELF ON AN ITTY BITTY SCALE. SO, IF IT HELPS, START THINKING OF THAT

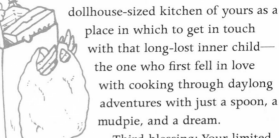

dollhouse-sized kitchen of yours as a place in which to get in touch with that long-lost inner child— the one who first fell in love with cooking through daylong adventures with just a spoon, a mudpie, and a dream.

Third blessing: Your limited storage space means you will need to market more frequently for smaller quantities, so from now on your food will always be much fresher and more carefully considered. It also means that marketing will become an increasingly interesting part of your everyday life— just as it is in all those films and books about living beautifully in the south of France.

Yes indeed—small is beautiful.

A New Way of Thinking about Groceries and Meals

IF YOU HAVE LIVED WITH YOUR IBK FOR SOME TIME, you have probably noticed that, dedicated though you may be to the idea of home economy and eating well, you have a fairly low kitchen "shut-off point"—the point, that is, at which any cooking at all just seems like too much trouble, and instead you pick up the phone to order in. If you live in a city of many good and inexpensive restaurants, have little free time, don't like food shopping, and are not an experienced day-to-day cook, your shut-off point is going to be appreciably lower than that of the general population. Even more so if you live alone.

Recognizing that this is the situation, consider now the possibility of shopping for simple meals that actually fall *within* your shut-off point rather than larger and more elaborate meals you admire on television and in magazines but will *never actually cook*.

Now give yourself permission to shop accordingly. That is, allow yourself to buy and eat foods that might cost a little more, but that will require much less preparation. And, at the same time, commit to doing a little bit of preparation of grocery items when you return home from the market, so that these smaller portions are available to you when you want them in individual-serving sizes.

One way of reconciling your inherently thrifty nature with these new groceries (not Lean Cuisine, but rather a number of higher-grade, easier-to-prepare cuts of meat and poultry, and also some relatively ready-to-eat foods in the tradition of French charcuterie) will be by recognizing that these new things will *actually* fit into your kitchen and you will *actually* make meals of them. Another way might be by recognizing that a larger "economy-sized" amount of food is no bargain if you don't really like it and half of it spoils before you get around to eating it.

Quite apart from changing the type and amount of food you bring into your small home, you might also want to consider the notion that singles and couples coping with minuscule and otherwise challenging kitchens *really are entitled* to cook and eat differently from people in larger, more rationally designed homes. Some nights we of the tiny-homed tribe want to make a meal that requires real focus and preparation, because doing so is a form of relaxation and amusement. Some nights we will go all out to entertain however many people can fit around our table or through our front door. But other nights, we just can't face the many challenges of that tiny little kitchen, so we just pop something in the toaster oven, pour ourselves a drink, and make up an appetizing little cold plate out of tapas-type things that are waiting for us there in the fridge.

The important thing to recognize about each of these ways of eating is that all are perfectly valid, and all can be perfectly healthful and satisfying, but you can't do *any* of them if you haven't got the right groceries on hand. So begin your new cooking adventure by doing a very serious reevaluation of your shopping habits. By stocking your little kitchen with foods appropriate to the way in which you really do prefer to eat, and developing some new, streamlined food preparation habits (starting with the ones in the next chapter), you too can rise above the natural single-person inclination to order in! That's right—because the high-quality food in your fridge will be (1) convenient, (2) delicious, and (3) ready and waiting for you with minimal preparation the moment you get home. Yes— *you won't even need to pick up the phone.*

Wrapping It Up

YOU WILL PROBABLY WANT to rewrap some of your groceries for refrigerator or freezer storage, just to ensure that you have portions better

I f you are just starting out in a new kitchen and know you need spices but don't know which ones, here is a good set to start out with. Clip this page and bring it with you to the market.

ALL SPICE BERRIES (whole)   GINGER (ground)

ANCHO CHILI POWDER   NUTMEG (WHOLE)

BAY LEAVES   OLD BAY SEASONING

CARAWAY SEEDS   OREGANO

CAYENNE   PEPPERCORNS (BLACK whole)

CHILI POWDER   RED PEPPER FLAKES

CINNAMON (GROUND)   ROSEMARY

CINNAMON (STICK)   SAFFRON

CLOVES (WHOLE)   SAGE

CUMIN (ground)   SEA SALT (COARSE)

CURRY POWDER   SWEET HUNGARIAN PAPRIKA

DRY ENGLISH MUSTARD   TABLE SALT

FENNEL SEEDS   THYME

suited to your needs. If so, self-locking plastic storage bags are probably best for the job (just squeeze all the air out of the bag), although a newly designed Press 'n Seal plastic storage wrap is also very good for sealing food airtight. Particularly if you are placing foods in the freezer, remove all extra air from the bag before sealing to prevent the oxidation of food surfaces and to lessen the possibility of freezer burn. If you are working with raw fish, meats, or poultry, wrap them in wax paper or freezer paper before putting them in a plastic bag—doing so will make later thawing and cooking much easier. Cheeses that are cut to order, whether frozen or not, also benefit from being wrapped in paper before being wrapped in plastic: mold-causing moisture won't collect on the surface of the cheese as it may with plastic wrap alone.

The freezer, incidentally, is a mysterious place. Many a crusty bachelor has wondered why his ice cube trays should enter the freezer full of fresh water but eventually produce shrunken, half-sized cubes tasting so oddly of garlic. This eerie phenomenon is the result of frost-free technology, which removes humidity from the freezer in order to prevent frosty buildup—and in so doing circulates air (and food odors) throughout the freezer compartment, dehydrating foods and ice cubes into the bargain. To minimize odor transfer and prevent dehydration, wrap foods for freezing carefully and tightly, keep an opened box of baking soda in the freezer to catch and neutralize odors, and make yourself fresh ice cubes on a weekly basis—or whenever you think of it—since there is nothing more ruinous to good (expensive) liquor than bad-tasting (inexpensive) ice.

6

When YOU PRESIDE OVER A SMALL KITCHEN, SIMPLICITY IS NOT SO MUCH AN AESTHETIC OR GASTRONOMIC CHOICE AS IT IS A PRACTICAL AND LOGISTICAL ONE. YET, WHILE THE SMALL-KITCHEN COOK HAS A STRONGER NEED FOR SIMPLE RECIPES THAN MOST, WE ALL WANT TO COOK INTERESTING FOOD, BECAUSE THAT'S THE FUN OF COOKING. SO GOOD RECIPES FOR SMALL KITCHENS ARE ONES THAT FEATURE THE COMBINED IMPERATIVES OF (1) BEING BREATHTAKINGLY SIMPLE AND (2) BEING INTERESTING ENOUGH TO MERIT THE TROUBLE OF COOKING. THE SEARCH FOR THE PERFECT RECIPE FOR THE IBK IS THEREFORE LIKE THE SEARCH FOR THE PERFECT LITTLE BLACK DRESS, SIZED PETITE: ENDLESS, AND ENDLESSLY INTERESTING—BUT ONLY IF PETITE IS YOUR SIZE.

| INSTANT COOKBOOK HOLDER! |

f you have trouble keeping a small cookbook (like this one) open and off your very small countertop, try suspending it in midair using a hinged trouser hanger. Put the opened book in the hanger, close the hinge, and hang up the cookbook on a cabinet door or cabinet top to keep it open and visible. If you have a favorite height and place for reading recipes, consider mounting a removable hook (suction-cup version, or a large-sized 3M "Command" removable hook) at just that spot.

The recipes that follow provide a number of different absurdly easy, tidy ways of preparing food by highlighting shortcuts more necessary to small kitchens than large ones (but they work in large ones, too). Use these recipes as a starting point, then become more ambitious as you grow in small-space self-assurance and corner-cutting techniques. Recipes that are great for entertaining carry the symbol. Just remember, always, that cooking overload occurs *much more quickly* in small kitchens than in large ones—so even if you're a seasoned cook, set your sights accordingly in this new, smaller space of yours, and always budget just a little more time and energy for meal preparation than you ever thought you'd need.

Finally, before entering that little kitchen of yours, consider practicing a favorite relaxation technique (deep breathing, creative visualization, yoga stretching) since your stress level will increase exponentially as your cooking space shrinks.

BREAKFAST THINGS

Most of us just grab something quick on the way to work, but a good homemade breakfast is often nutritionally better for you, and really very simple, once you get the hang of making it. Here are some fast, easy things to try for breakfast, plus a couple more elaborate ideas for the weekend.

For other breakfast dishes, see Quiche the Easy Way on page 124 and Quiche the Hard Way on page 126. Also consider using a boxed corn bread mix to make a fast 8 × 8-inch pan of corn bread in your toaster oven; see the flavor variations outlined in One-Pot, No-Mess Corn Bread on page 162.

This is an incredibly fast, easy, and good way of making 2 eggs for breakfast with no watching or standing around. No sticking either. Take a shower while they cook, using a timer so you'll get the yolks cooked just right.

SERVES 1

NONSTICK COOKING SPRAY (OR A LITTLE UNSALTED BUTTER OR OLIVE OIL)

1 THIN SLICE HAM (SERRANO, PROSCIUTTO, OR WHATEVER YOU'VE GOT)

1 OR 2 LARGE EGGS, AS DESIRED

1 TABLESPOON CREAM, UNSALTED BUTTER, AND/OR GRATED CHEESE

PREHEAT YOUR OVEN OR TOASTER OVEN to 350 degrees F.

Spray, butter, or oil an 8-ounce ramekin or custard cup. Put in the ham slice, break an egg (or 2 eggs) on top, and then put the cream, butter, or cheese, or any combination of these, on top of the egg(s). Bake for 12 minutes for 1 egg, 17 minutes for 2 eggs. To serve, grasp the ham by the edge and slip the ham and egg out of the custard cup and onto a plate—or else just eat it tidily from the cup.

Nonstick Cooking Spray Tip: While nonstick spray is great at keeping food from sticking, it can create an aerosol mess on your kitchen countertops. So to contain any unwanted oily mess, before spraying, place your dish in the sink (or the inside door of your dishwasher, if you have one).

STEEL-CUT OATMEAL

Steel-cut oatmeal tastes a whole lot better than processed instant oatmeal, and though it takes a while to cook, it can be made in a big batch and stored in a quart container in the refrigerator. Unlike instant rolled oats, it reheats beautifully on the stovetop or in the microwave, so if you make one batch at the beginning of the week, you can eat it all week long with very little pot-watching. It is also more compact than rolled oats: You need just $^1/_4$ cup to make yourself a bowl. Buy it economically (in bulk) at whole foods stores.
Serve with honey, syrup, dark brown sugar, or jam, and some butter and/or raisins if desired.

MAKES 4 CUPS

4 CUPS WATER
1 CUP STEEL-CUT OATS

BRING THE WATER TO A BOIL in a medium nonstick saucepan, add the oatmeal, return to a boil, lower the flame, and cook over low heat for 30 minutes, stirring occasionally.

NOTE: For an alternative, overnight method: Cook oatmeal as above, but after returning it to a boil, turn off the heat, cover it, and leave it overnight. Reheat it briefly in the morning either on the stovetop or in the microwave, adding a small amount of additional water if necessary.

A smoothie is a fast, easy way of drinking *breakfast for those who don't like eating in the morning. The following recipe makes 2 smoothies: one to drink for breakfast, and one to keep in the refrigerator as an afternoon pick-me-up. Cooked oatmeal may sound like an improbable ingredient for a shake, but it works well as a thickener and provides soluble fiber and complex carbohydrates— both are important to starting the day right and keeping you from sudden attacks of hunger. (If you've tried the Steel-Cut Oatmeal recipe on page 81, you may just have some cold cooked oatmeal waiting in the refrigerator.)*

SERVES 2

ONE 6-OUNCE CONTAINER YOGURT OF CHOICE

6 OUNCES ORANGE JUICE (YOU CAN USE THE YOGURT CONTAINER TO MEASURE)

$3/4$ CUP COOKED OATMEAL, INSTANT OR STEEL-CUT (YOU CAN USE THE YOGURT CONTAINER TO MEASURE)

1 TABLESPOON HONEY, OR TO TASTE

1 BANANA, OR 1 YOGURT CONTAINER OF INDIVIDUALLY QUICK-FROZEN OR FRESH BLUEBERRIES OR RASPBERRIES

1 LARGE EGG (OPTIONAL)

6 ICE CUBES

PUT ALL THE INGREDIENTS except for the ice cubes in your blender and mix thoroughly. Then add the ice cubes one at a time and blend on highest speed until the ice is pulverized.

Blender Cleanup Tip: You don't need to take your blender apart after every use. For fastest cleanup, fill the freshly used blender halfway with hot water, add a few drops of dish soap, put the cover on, blend on high for 30 seconds, and then simply rinse clean with hot water.

SOUPS

Simple soups are great for small kitchens since they are easy, satisfying, and make your house feel very homey. Canned soups to which you make a few improvements are also very good. I include several of both here, because sometimes you have the time to make soup from scratch, and sometimes you just *don't*. If you eat canned soup often, try to find the low-sodium varieties, and feel free to improve them on your own through the addition of frozen vegetables, chopped fresh parsley or chives, freshly squeezed lemon juice, or even just a little bit of cider vinegar or tarragon vinegar. Keep in mind also that all of the homemade soups in this section freeze well in single-serving containers and heat up in minutes on the stovetop or in the microwave. (One final soup recipe, Scotch Broth, Irish Style, can be found as a variation on the Stovetop Irish Stew on page 103.)

HOMEMADE (!) SPLIT PEA SOUP

*Although a real split pea soup is traditionally made with
gristly smoked ham hocks, which must be picked apart by hand,
there is a simpler way.
Top your pea soup with homemade garlicky croutons
(see recipe page 87), which are a particularly good addition
if you serve the soup puréed.*

SERVES 6

3 SHALLOTS, FINELY CHOPPED, OR 1 MEDIUM ONION, FINELY CHOPPED

3 TABLESPOONS UNSALTED BUTTER, DUCK FAT, LARD, OR OLIVE OIL

2 CUPS DRIED GREEN SPLIT PEAS, RINSED AND PICKED OVER

6 CUPS LOW-SODIUM CHICKEN OR BEEF BROTH

FINELY GROUND BLACK PEPPER

1 BAY LEAF

$^1/_2$ CUP CHOPPED SMITHFIELD OR COUNTRY HAM

1 MEDIUM POTATO, PEELED AND DICED

IN A DUTCH OVEN OR MEDIUM LIDDED CASSEROLE, cook the shallots or
onion gently in the fat until translucent. Add the split peas, broth,
pepper, bay leaf, ham, and potato. Bring the mixture to a boil, then
lower the flame and simmer gently for 1 hour, stirring occasionally
to prevent scorching (a nonstick pot works best here) and adding
water as needed if the mixture seems too dry and thick.

(continued)

When the soup is done, taste it, adjust the seasoning, and remove the bay leaf. Mash up the soup a little with a potato masher if you like a thicker soup. If you want a creamy soup, use an immersion blender or purée a cup or two in a blender and return it to the pot—but wash out your blender soon after, because pea soup dries quickly and forever. (See the Blender Cleanup Tip on page 83 for easiest cleaning.)

 This is a good dish for a dinner party.

NOTE: To make a more substantial meal: Add one or two sliced premium-quality frankfurters per person and heat them through in the soup.

Croutons

A very busy friend whose cupboard contains little more than cornflakes and canned split pea soup once remarked to me that if you make homemade croutons for the latter, everyone will think you're a great cook.

SERVES 6

6 tablespoons olive oil
3 garlic cloves, sliced thin
6 slices white bread, crusts removed, cut into $1/2$-inch cubes
Salt

Heat the oil in a nonstick sauté pan. When the oil is hot, add the garlic and fry it until golden, then remove. Add the bread cubes and stir, frying them until golden as well, shaking the pan to move the cubes around. When they are brown all over, remove the pan from the heat, sprinkle them with salt to taste, and either drain and cool the croutons on paper towels or else just serve them from the pan. Leftover croutons (though I never seem to have any) can be refrigerated in a small container or plastic bag for later use—reheated briefly, if desired, at 300 degrees F.

Miso paste lasts almost indefinitely in the refrigerator and is great when you need a warm and restorative pick-me-up—it's particularly good for a cold, a hangover, or both.

SERVES 2

2 CUPS LOW-SODIUM CHICKEN BROTH

1 TABLESPOON RED OR WHITE MISO PASTE

1 SCALLION, FINELY MINCED

IN A SMALL SAUCEPAN, heat the broth to boiling, then turn off the heat. In a small bowl, whisk the miso with a couple of tablespoons of the hot broth. Stir this mixture into the rest of the broth, pour into bowls, and top with the minced scallion.

This is a substantial enough soup that it makes a very good, easy meal—a pasta dish, in other words, without a rich or heavy sauce.

SERVES 1 AS A MAIN COURSE; 2 AS A STARTER

1 $1/2$ CUPS FRESH OR FROZEN TORTELLINI

2 CUPS LOW-SODIUM CHICKEN BROTH

HALF A 10-OUNCE PACKAGE FROZEN CHOPPED SPINACH,
    COOKED AND SQUEEZED DRY

A GRATING OF FRESH NUTMEG

FRESHLY GRATED PARMESAN CHEESE

COOK THE TORTELLINI AS DIRECTED in a 1-quart saucepan and drain it. Heat the broth in a small saucepan. Add the spinach to the broth, sprinkle on the grated nutmeg, and stir. Place the tortellini in a bowl and pour the broth over it. To serve, top with the grated cheese.

This recipe makes a nice, dark, thick, rich, and (optionally) vegetarian soup—one so thick that it's almost a stew.

SERVES 4

2 TO 4 OUNCES DRIED PORCINI MUSHROOMS

TWO 10-OUNCE BOXES WHITE MUSHROOMS

2 TABLESPOONS UNSALTED BUTTER

2 TABLESPOONS OLIVE OIL

SALT

FRESHLY GROUND BLACK PEPPER

1 SHALLOT, FINELY CHOPPED

1 GARLIC CLOVE, FINELY CHOPPED

4 CUPS LOW-SODIUM CHICKEN BROTH OR VEGETABLE BROTH

$^1/_4$ CUP PEARL BARLEY

SOUR CREAM (OPTIONAL)

MINCED CHIVES (OPTIONAL)

SOAK THE PORCINI MUSHROOMS in 2 cups of boiling water for 15 minutes. Reserving the soaking liquid, drain the mushrooms, rinse them of grit under running water, and chop them. Strain the mushroom liquid through a paper coffee filter to remove any additional sand and grit.

Wipe clean and slice the white mushrooms (a sturdy egg slicer, if you have one, does this very quickly). Sauté them in a $3^1/2$-quart saucepan in the butter and olive oil, sprinkling them with salt and pepper to taste; cook them until brown. Add the shallot and garlic and cook until fragrant, not letting them brown or burn. Add the chicken broth, the porcini mushrooms, and the reserved soaking liquid, and bring the mixture to a simmer. Add the barley and cook for another 40 minutes, adding more water or broth if the mixture gets too thick.

Serve as is, or with a spoonful of sour cream and a sprinkling of chives if desired.

*A good friend of mine, the Brazilian television host and journalist
Lucia Guimaraes, refers to this recipe as "fake feijoada" after the great
and elaborate black bean party dish that she enjoys preparing for large
groups of friends. She suggests garnishing this home-alone version in
the Rio de Janeiro style: that is, with bits of peeled and chopped fresh
orange. A sprinkling of freshly toasted bread crumbs can create an
approximation of the traditional Brazilian topping for feijoada—
farofa, or toasted manioc flour.*

SERVES 2

1 SHALLOT, FINELY CHOPPED, OR 1 SMALL ONION, FINELY CHOPPED

2 TABLESPOONS OLIVE OIL

1 GARLIC CLOVE, FINELY CHOPPED

PINCH OF DRIED OREGANO

ONE 15^1/2-OUNCE CAN BLACK BEAN SOUP

1 TABLESPOON RED WINE VINEGAR

^{1}/3 CUP DICED SPANISH CHORIZO (1^1/2 OUNCES)

FLESH OF ^{1}/2 ORANGE, FINELY CHOPPED

1 TABLESPOON FINELY CHOPPED FRESH CILANTRO (OPTIONAL)

HOT SAUCE (OPTIONAL)

FRESHLY TOASTED BREAD CRUMBS OR CRACKER CRUMBS (OPTIONAL)

IN A MEDIUM SAUCEPAN, sauté the shallot in the olive oil until fragrant, then add the garlic and cook for 2 minutes more, being careful not to let the garlic brown. Add the oregano, rubbing it between your fingers a bit as you do so, and stir. Then add the soup, vinegar, and chorizo, and bring the mixture to a boil. Reduce heat and let it simmer for 5 minutes or longer. Serve the soup in bowls, and top it with chopped fresh orange, cilantro, if desired, hot sauce to taste, and toasted bread crumbs.

To one 15-ounce can of New England–style clam chowder, add the suggested amount of milk, half-and-half, or cream, and one 10-ounce can of chopped clams and their juice. Heat the mixture through. A piece of cooked bacon, crumbled, makes a good garnish, but so does a pat of unsalted butter with much less trouble. Some finely chopped fresh parsley or chives makes a pretty green addition to the white chowder and yellow butter. Serve, however garnished, with oyster crackers, common crackers, or saltines.

MAIN COURSES

Cooking dinner at home, particularly if you live in a city full of ethnic variety, seems to me to be mostly about making foods that are comfortable, familiar, and easy to digest. Sometimes you will want to make a proper meal with meat and two vegetables, and sometimes you will want just a one-bowl or one-plate affair that you can eat while watching TV. Here are a variety of simply seasoned main courses, all of which cook up easily using very few dishes. All reheat well, too, so even if you live alone, you can make them in full-sized quantities and have some great, sturdy leftovers. And some are great for entertaining.

Meat loaf seems complicated (to me) to make, but this version doesn't require much chopping, which can be difficult in tight spaces. You can feed four people with this meat loaf and still have lots left—an important point, since meat loaf is the ultimate *leftover. It makes great sandwiches (on buttered toast, with watercress, ketchup, mustard, and/or mayo) and also reheats beautifully in a low (300 degrees F) oven, wrapped in a piece of foil. If you are feeling adventurous, you can also spread slices of leftover meat loaf thinly with ketchup and broil them (but watch closely or they'll burn).*

Meat loaf mix (1 pound chopped beef, $^1/_2$ pound chopped veal, $^1/_2$ pound chopped pork) is sold packaged at most supermarkets.

SERVES 4, WITH LEFTOVERS

1 LARGE SHALLOT OR SMALL ONION

3 SCALLIONS, TRIMMED

2 GARLIC CLOVES

ONE 7-OUNCE JAR ROASTED RED PEPPERS (PIMIENTOS)

2 LARGE EGGS

$^1/_3$ CUP LOW-SODIUM BEEF OR CHICKEN BROTH

1 TABLESPOON WORCESTERSHIRE SAUCE

1 TABLESPOON TABASCO SAUCE

2 TABLESPOONS SOY SAUCE

2 POUNDS MEAT LOAF MIX

1 CUP SHREDDED MONTEREY JACK CHEESE (4 OUNCES)

3/4 CUP CRACKER MEAL OR CRUSHED SALTINES

1 TO 3 TABLESPOONS KETCHUP

5 SLICES BACON, CUT IN HALF

PREHEAT YOUR OVEN OR TOASTER OVEN to 350 degrees F.

Chop the shallot and scallions and then mince the garlic. Drain the roasted peppers and chop them, too. In a mixing bowl large enough to hold all the ingredients, beat the eggs and add the broth, Worcestershire, Tabasco, and soy sauce (if you plan on using crushed saltines and are worried about salt, reduce the soy sauce to 1 tablespoon). Now add the chopped vegetables, the meat loaf mix, the Jack cheese, and the cracker meal. Mix everything together thoroughly using your (clean) hands and enjoy the extreme cold mushiness of the experience.

Pat the meat loaf into an 8 × 8-inch ovenproof baking dish (line the dish with tinfoil if desired; see the tip that follows). Top this mixture with a very thin layer of ketchup (no more, or it will throw off the flavor of the dish) and then with the bacon. Bake the meat loaf for 90 minutes. Let the meat loaf stand on a cooling rack for at least 10 minutes before slicing.

Meat Loaf Cleanup and Storage Tip: If you intend to store the meat loaf in the same pan in which you've cooked it (and it's very convenient to do so, particularly if you have a rubberized lid for your 8 × 8-inch pan), consider lining the pan with tinfoil before cooking. At the end of your meal, lift the meat loaf out of the dish, pour off any liquid, and place the meat loaf into the clean dish. (If you don't line the dish with tinfoil, the pan will need some scrubbing, thanks to cooked-on ketchup.)

Saltine-Crushing Tip: If you need to crush saltines to make the meat loaf, you can improvise a mortar and pestle by using a large stoneware mug as the mortar and a glass spice bottle (washed and dried) as the pestle. The saltines will crumble perfectly and all the crumbs will stay in the mug.

Here is an ultra-simple pot roast (made with a miraculously inexpensive cut of beef) that is incredibly *delicious—dark, rich, and fork-tender. Its slow cooking makes your entire home smell beefy and good. By using a boneless chuck steak rather than chuck roast, you don't even need to carve or slice anything—it's ready to go to the plate just as it is.*

Mom's final note to me on this recipe: "Make gravy or not depending on your mood and degree of hunger." I am not a gravy-making guy (and neither is Mom—who is she kidding?), so while I might use sour cream (or applesauce) mixed with prepared horseradish as an accompaniment, I find this pot roast is really delicious all by itself, garnished with just a little finely chopped fresh parsley.

SERVES 2

$1^1/2$ TO 2 POUNDS BONELESS CHUCK STEAK, ABOUT $1^1/2$ INCHES THICK, WITH SOME FAT ON IT

SALT

FRESHLY GROUND BLACK PEPPER

2 SHALLOTS, OR 1 MEDIUM-LARGE ONION, PEELED BUT LEFT WHOLE

$1/3$ CUP LOW-SODIUM BEEF BROTH (OPTIONAL)

2 MEDIUM POTATOES, PEELED AND CUT INTO CHUNKS

3 MEDIUM CARROTS, SCRAPED AND CUT INTO CHUNKS

(continued)

PREHEAT YOUR (TOASTER) OVEN to 375 degrees F.

Line a 9 × 9-inch pan with tinfoil for easiest cleanup. Season the meat well with salt and pepper and put it in the pan with the shallots or onion. Add $^1/_3$ cup of water or the broth if using. Put the pan in the oven uncovered and roast for 30 minutes.

Turn the meat over, cover the pan with foil, and bake for 30 to 45 minutes more at a reduced heat of 350 degrees F. Add the potatoes and carrots to the pan, turning and basting them with the juices as you do so and sprinkling them with some salt and pepper. Then cover the pan again with the aluminum foil and bake until the vegetables are done—about 30 minutes more.

Chateaubriand, the center cut of a filet of beef, is about the most elegant thing to be found on a cow. It's also the simplest to cook, and you can serve it barely warm, so it is perfect for dinner parties. Use your toaster oven and amaze your friends.

Cooking the roast to the exactly right temperature and for exactly the right amount of time is crucial, so make sure your oven is preheated and your oven temperature is correct, and have an instant-read thermometer on hand to check the roast for doneness. Also make sure your oven is clean, because high-temperature cooking of this sort can make dirty ovens (even itty bitty ones) smoke.

Serve these thick slices on a platter garnished with watercress, accompanied by either Dijon mustard, a simple sauce of sour cream mixed with prepared horseradish to taste, or Blender Béarnaise (page 151). Two sauces will give the meal a feeling of extra luxury. Asparagus, also at room temperature, makes a great accompaniment to this roast, as does Baked Potato (page 155), which will give a needed warmth to the meal.

SERVES 4, WITH LEFTOVERS

1 CHATEAUBRIAND (ABOUT 2 POUNDS), TRIMMED AND TIED

OLIVE OIL

SALT

FRESHLY GROUND BLACK PEPPER

(continued)

PREHEAT YOUR TOASTER OVEN to 450 degrees F.

Rub the meat lightly with olive oil and sprinkle it with salt and pepper to taste.

Place the meat in an 8 × 8-inch or 9 × 9-inch baking dish (in an 8 × 8-inch dish you may have to place the roast on a diagonal).

Roast the beef for about 20 minutes, or until an instant-read thermometer registers 125 degrees F. Remove the roast from the oven and let it sit for 15 minutes to cool. At serving time, remove the strings and slice into pieces about $1^1/2$ inches thick.

NOTE Leftover chateaubriand, sliced thin, makes a great sandwich, particularly on toasted white bread with a few pieces of watercress and leftover béarnaise.

STOVETOP IRISH STEW

Very easy—all you do is simmer it. If you have hungry guests on hand, they will be reassured by the good, hearty smell created by this stew just as soon as it comes to a boil—thus keeping everyone calm and cheerful during a slightly prolonged cocktail hour (in which you, too, are entirely free to take part!).

SERVES 4

3 LARGE POTATOES, PEELED

3 MEDIUM ONIONS, SLICED THIN

2 POUNDS BONELESS LAMB STEW MEAT, CUT INTO CHUNKS

SALT

FRESHLY GROUND BLACK PEPPER

1 TABLESPOON WORCESTERSHIRE SAUCE

1 BAY LEAF

2 GARLIC CLOVES, FINELY CHOPPED

$2^1/2$ CUPS LOW-SODIUM BEEF BROTH

2 MEDIUM CARROTS, SCRAPED AND CUT INTO CHUNKS

2 TABLESPOONS FINELY CHOPPED FRESH PARSLEY

JUICE OF $^1/2$ LEMON

SLICE 1 POTATO THINLY. Leave the other 2 potatoes to soak in cold water. Put the sliced potato and onions into a Dutch oven along with the lamb. Sprinkle salt and pepper over the lamb, potatoes, and onions. Add the Worcestershire, bay leaf, garlic, and broth. Cover, bring to a boil, then lower heat and simmer gently for 45 minutes.

Cut the remaining 2 potatoes into chunks and add them along with the carrots and 1 tablespoon of the parsley. Cook for 45 minutes more, then add the lemon juice and stir. Taste; add more salt and pepper and more lemon juice if necessary. Sprinkle the stew with the remaining parsley and serve it straight from the Dutch oven into bowls, accompanied by crusty French bread.

Irish stew refrigerates and reheats well, but don't freeze it: the potatoes become mushy.

VARIATION: SCOTCH BROTH, IRISH STYLE Omit the 2 potatoes in chunks, and instead, during the last 45 minutes of cooking, add $^3/_4$ cup pearl barley and an additional 2 cups of broth. If you'd like a more delicate soup, you may cut the lamb into smaller pieces.

A 7-ounce cured ham steak, which is available precut and packaged at the market (and will live a very long time that way in the back of your refrigerator or in your freezer) is easily browned in a nonstick omelet pan with a little melted unsalted butter over gentle heat. Just remove the rind first (or prepare to chew a little bit more). Serve the ham with cranberry sauce, chutney, Quick Cumberland Sauce (page 152), or Dijon mustard. Mustard greens, kale, or lima beans make a delicious accompaniment.

VARIATION: HAM STEAK WITH EGG After removing the ham from the pan as directed above, quickly fry an egg (or 2 eggs) in a tablespoon of unsalted butter in the same pan, and serve it atop the ham slice, with a sprinkling of chopped chives. With 1 egg, this serves 1 hungry person; with 2 eggs, it feeds 2 "regular" people.

Chops (lamb, pork, veal) are a staple of small-kitchen cookery and a top meal choice for bachelors everywhere. (Note that a lamb chop recipe follows.) Standard thick chops at most supermarkets are 2 inches thick; if possible, speak to your butcher and get extra-thick chops, about 3 inches thick.

You can brine your pork chops to keep them extra juicy (as described in the accompanying sidebar), but in any case plan to serve them with some sort of fruit sauce (cranberry sauce, applesauce, or chutney), a simple pan sauce, or a highly flavored side dish, since these roasted chops are very simply seasoned.

SERVES 2

2 REALLY THICK PORK CHOPS (ABOUT 10 OUNCES FOR THICK CHOPS, 14 TO 16 OUNCES FOR EXTRA THICK)

SALT

FRESHLY GROUND BLACK PEPPER

BROTH OR WHITE WINE, IF NEEDED

PREHEAT YOUR OVEN OR TOASTER OVEN to 350 degrees F.

Place a nonstick skillet over low heat (or, if you don't mind a little smoke, medium heat). If you have brined the chops, pat them dry. If you have not, sprinkle the chops with salt. Place the chops in the heated skillet and cook for 5 minutes on each side, just to give them a little color. (Alternatively, skip this step entirely and reconcile yourself to eating a gray chop.)

Place the chops in an 8 × 8-inch baking dish. Sprinkle them with pepper. Bake for 1 hour, then remove and check with an instant-read thermometer. The chop is done when the pork reaches 150 degrees F; depending on the thickness of the chop, this will take anywhere from 60 to 90 minutes. If at any point the dish starts to smoke, add enough water, broth, or white wine to cover the bottom of the dish. (These pan juices, enriched with 2 tablespoons of un-salted butter or cream, are good poured over the chop at serving time.)

(continued)

| WHY BRINE PORK CHOPS? |

Brining—soaking in cold salt water—seals the surface of the pork so the juices can't leak out while the chops cook. It really does make a big difference with pork, which nowadays is bred for leanness, aka dryness. For the simplest possible brining solution, dissolve 2 tablespoons of salt in 2 cups of cool water. Place 1 or 2 chops in a sealable container (either a locking plastic bag or a lidded dish) and pour the salt water over, adding a bit more water if necessary to cover the chops. Seal and refrigerate for 1 hour (no longer or the pork will become too salty to eat). When you are ready to cook the chops, remove them from the liquid and pat them dry with paper towels.

VARIATION: PORK CHOPS WITH APRICOT GLAZE Make a quick glaze consisting of 2 tablespoons apricot jam, 2 tablespoons dark brown sugar, 1 tablespoon cider vinegar, 1 teaspoon dry mustard, $^1/_4$ teaspoon ground cinnamon, $^1/_8$ teaspoon ground cloves, and 1 teaspoon Tabasco.

Make the chops as described above, but line the baking dish with nonstick foil. After browning the pork chops, spoon the glaze over them. Bake as instructed. When the chops are cooked to 150 degrees F, switch the toaster oven from "bake" to "broil" and broil until the glaze is bubbling and gooey, about 5 minutes. Let the chops cool a bit before eating.

Spice Grinding Tip: If you need to grind up spices such as cloves, cumin, or allspice berries, you can improvise a mortar and pestle by using a stoneware mug as the mortar and a glass spice bottle (washed and dried) as the pestle.

I f your toaster oven comes in for heavy use—that is, if you use it to roast chops and other delectables—the interior is eventually going to get dirty. Since this little appliance takes pride of place in your kitchen, keep it looking fine. Here's how.

Unplug the appliance. Remove the crumb tray if there is one. Remove the foil you have used to line the crumb tray and wash the crumb tray. Wipe out the inside of the toaster oven using a sponge or damp cloth soaked in mild detergent and hot water. In case of sticky spots, drips, and incinerated food, use a damp cloth and some baking soda as a mild abrasive. After the soap solution, use glass cleaner to clean the toaster oven window streak-free. Wipe dry the interior, place a new piece of foil in the crumb tray, return the crumb tray to the toaster oven, and there you are—it's as pretty as the day that you bought it.

TOASTER-OVEN LAMB CHOPS

A thick loin lamb chop will broil up quickly and neatly in your toaster oven. Just make sure your chops are the dense, nearly cubic loin chops, not the long, flat rib or blade chops. Serve 2 chops per person (you can usually cook 8 at a time in most toaster ovens). Mint jelly (or mint sauce) is the traditional accompaniment, but lamb is so flavorful that a simple squeeze of lemon works equally well. Lamb chops are good served over watercress or arugula.

SERVES 2

4 LOIN LAMB CHOPS, 1^1/2 TO 2 INCHES THICK (ABOUT 6 OUNCES)
SALT
FRESHLY GROUND BLACK PEPPER

PREHEAT THE BROILER OF YOUR TOASTER OVEN and make sure that the rack is in the "up" position to bring the chops up as close as possible to the heat source.

Sprinkle the chops with salt and pepper and place them in a roasting dish. Broil the chops for 6 minutes, then turn and broil for another 6 minutes for medium-rare. That's it—all done.

ROAST BONELESS CENTER-CUT LOIN OF PORK

This is one of the great, easy, inexpensive cuts of all time. A center cut is uniformly thick and needs no rolling or tying. It cooks beautifully in a toaster oven and makes a great small dinner party meal. If you are cooking for 1 or 2, you can cook the entire roast at once and have plenty left over for sandwiches and casseroles; or, you can very easily slice the raw roast in half and freeze the remainder for another time. This cut is very mild in flavor, so it responds well to any spice rub you might care to use on it; the relatively simple rub suggested here is best if you intend to use leftovers for other recipes (such as stir-fries and casseroles) or for sandwiches.

SERVES 6

1 BONELESS CENTER-CUT PORK LOIN (ABOUT 3 POUNDS)

OLIVE OIL

SALT

FRESHLY GROUND BLACK PEPPER

1 TEASPOON DRIED OREGANO

2 GARLIC CLOVES CUT INTO SLIVERS (OPTIONAL)

6 SHALLOTS, PEELED, TRIMMED, AND RUBBED WITH OLIVE OIL (OPTIONAL)

PREHEAT YOUR (TOASTER) OVEN to 450 degrees F.

Rub the roast with olive oil and sprinkle it generously with salt, pepper, and oregano. Insert slivers of garlic into the roast if you like, using a paring knife to make the incisions. Place the meat in a 9 × 9-inch baking dish lined with nonstick foil (along with the shallots if you would like them as an accompaniment) and roast for 10 minutes. Reduce the heat to 250 degrees F and roast for 1 hour and 15 minutes more. At this point test the roast with an instant-read thermometer: It should read 150 degrees F. If not, continue to cook the pork until it reaches this temperature. Remove from the oven and let the dish cool on a rack for 10 minutes, then transfer the roast to a cutting board. The easiest way to serve this roast is simply to slice it into chop-sized servings (about 1 inch thick).

CHICKEN AND RICE IN A POT

This is a very easy and satisfying one-pot stovetop meal—so much so that you may find yourself eating it every single night for a week, as I did when my nephew, Kelby, visited. The recipe can be doubled very easily for company. Although usually served hot, it can also be molded and served at room temperature with elegant arabesques of squeeze-bottle mayonnaise as decoration (Kelby's idea). Alternatively, add just a couple of other ingredients, and you can turn this one-pot wonder into a short-order paella.

SERVES 2

4 SKINLESS, BONELESS CHICKEN THIGHS (ABOUT 1 $^1/_2$ POUNDS)

$^1/_2$ CUP UNBLEACHED ALL-PURPOSE FLOUR

SALT

FRESHLY GROUND BLACK PEPPER

2 TABLESPOONS OLIVE OIL

2 SHALLOTS, FINELY CHOPPED, OR 1 ONION, FINELY CHOPPED

1 GARLIC CLOVE, MINCED

1 CUP LONG-GRAIN OR BASMATI RICE

$^1/_2$ CUP CHOPPED ROASTED RED PEPPERS (PIMIENTOS)

PINCH OF SAFFRON OR TURMERIC (OPTIONAL)

2 CUPS LOW-SODIUM CHICKEN BROTH, HEATED

$^1/_2$ CUP FROZEN PEAS (OPTIONAL)

LEMON WEDGES

2 TABLESPOONS CHOPPED FRESH PARSLEY OR CILANTRO

HOT SAUCE

CUT THE CHICKEN INTO BITE-SIZED CHUNKS and toss them in a plastic bag with the flour and salt and pepper to taste. Heat the olive oil in a small (1-quart) nonstick pot, and just before it begins to smoke, add the chicken and sauté in batches until brown, removing each batch to a bowl. Add the shallots to the pot and sauté until translucent. Then add the garlic, stir, and a moment later add the rice. Cook, stirring, over medium heat until the rice glistens and smells toasty. Then add the pimientos, the saffron or turmeric if using, and the browned chicken. Stir and then add the heated chicken broth. Stir briefly again, then cover and cook over low heat for about 30 minutes. (If you'd like to have peas in this dish, just pour them on top of the rice during the last 8 minutes of cooking.) Serve hot with lemon wedges and parsley or cilantro as an accompaniment, with hot sauce on the side.

Browning in Batches Tip: Rather than use a bowl to hold the cooked chicken as you brown it in batches, save yourself some washing up by removing the cooked chicken to the lid of the pot (since you'll need to use the lid to cook the rice anyway). Steady the lid by placing it on a bowl, if necessary.

(continued)

VARIATION: SUMMER CHICKEN AND RICE Let the chicken and rice cool slightly, then spoon it into a small mixing bowl (or individual serving bowls) lined with plastic wrap. Unmold the dish onto a platter and decorate the molded rice with artful squiggles of (squeeze-bottle) mayonnaise, garnishing with fresh parsley or cilantro and lemon wedges. A dollop of homemade mayonnaise (recipe on page 149) would also be great.

VARIATION: SHORT-ORDER PAELLA Add $^1/_2$ cup (about 2 ounces) diced Spanish chorizo to the rice as it sautés. Add an 8-ounce bag of thawed salad shrimp and 1 cup cooked peas atop the rice 7 minutes prior to serving, stirring to incorporate at the last minute. Turn the mixture out onto a serving platter and sprinkle with finely chopped fresh parsley or cilantro and fresh lemon juice.

Chicken and turkey cutlets are very fast and easy to cook, and sweet Marsala, an inexpensive fortified wine, makes a delicious and memorable instant sauce. If you are cooking for yourself alone, you might sauce only the cutlets you plan to eat right away and keep the remainder plain; they make great next-day sandwiches and are also very good on a cold plate with cranberry sauce, lingonberries, or Quick Cumberland Sauce (page 152). If you are concerned about vaporized grease in your kitchen, use a spatter screen here—but rest assured that the cooking doesn't go on for very long.
Enjoy the sauce created by this dish with rice, instant couscous, or just some crusty bread and salad.

SERVES 2

4 CHICKEN OR TURKEY BREAST CUTLETS (ABOUT 1 POUND)

$^1/_2$ CUP FRESHLY GRATED PARMESAN CHEESE

3 TABLESPOONS UNSALTED BUTTER

1 TABLESPOON PEANUT OR LIGHT OLIVE OIL

1 GARLIC CLOVE, PEELED AND LIGHTLY CRUSHED

$^1/_4$ CUP LOW-SODIUM BEEF BROTH

$^1/_4$ CUP SWEET MARSALA

FINELY CHOPPED FRESH PARSLEY OR CHIVES

WASH THE CUTLETS IN COOL WATER and pat them dry with a paper towel. (They really do need to be dry or else they will spatter.)

(continued)

Place the Parmesan in a plastic bag or on a plate. Add one cutlet at a time and coat with cheese.

Set your (toaster) oven to about 250 degrees F, and put a baking dish that will hold the finished cutlets into the (toaster) oven to warm.

In a sauté pan, heat the butter and oil together over moderate heat until the foam from the butter subsides. Then add the garlic and 2 cutlets. Cook each cutlet until it is light brown on both sides. Keep an eye on the garlic; if it gets too brown, remove and discard it. As your cutlets are done, place them in the heated dish and keep them warm in the oven. Continue until all the cutlets are done.

Then turn up the heat beneath the sauté pan, add the beef broth, and boil the liquid down until syrupy. Then add the Marsala and boil down once again until syrupy. Return the cutlets to the pan and turn them to coat with the sauce. Return the cutlets to the warmed baking dish and pour the rest of the sauce over them. Garnish with parsley or chives.

Splatter Tips: If you haven't got a splatter screen, you can improvise with a sieve. Just place the sieve over the sauté pan to lessen the amount of vaporized grease—and cleanup time. Keep your stovetop clean of splatters, meanwhile, by covering your unused burners with easy-to-clean burner covers.

Oven-fried chicken is delicious and easy, with no greasy spattering and no messy cleanup, which is perhaps why it was such a favorite among moms of the pre–Chicken McNugget generation. But real chicken breast is bland and dries out quickly—so the coating you use has to be rich and flavorful.

SERVES 4

4 SMALL SKINLESS, BONELESS CHICKEN BREASTS (ABOUT 1$^1/_2$ POUNDS), OR
    10 CHICKEN TENDERS (ABOUT 1 POUND)
$^1/_2$ CUP SOUR CREAM
1 GARLIC CLOVE, VERY FINELY CHOPPED OR MASHED
SALT
FRESHLY GROUND BLACK PEPPER
$^1/_2$ CUP DRIED SEASONED ITALIAN BREAD CRUMBS, CRACKER MEAL, OR CRUSHED SALTINES
$^1/_2$ CUP FRESHLY GRATED PARMESAN CHEESE, PLUS ADDITIONAL FOR SPRINKLING
CHOPPED FRESH PARSLEY
LEMON WEDGES

PREHEAT YOUR OVEN OR TOASTER OVEN to 350 degrees F.

Wash the chicken in cool water and pat it dry very thoroughly with paper towels (otherwise the sour cream will not stick).

Combine the chicken with the sour cream, garlic, and salt and pepper to taste in a small bowl and stir to coat. (If you are using crushed saltines, use less salt, and refer to the Saltine-Crushing Tip on page 98.)   *(continued)*

Place the bread crumbs, cracker meal, or crushed saltines and grated cheese in a shallow bowl and mix. Dip the chicken into the mixture and press to coat. Place the chicken pieces into your baking dish (they will fit into a 9 × 9-inch dish). Discard any remaining crumb mixture.

Bake the chicken for about 30 minutes for boneless breasts, 25 minutes for tenders. If you like a very brown crust on your chicken, switch the toaster oven to broil for the final 5 minutes. (Cracker meal and saltine crumbs will not brown as well as seasoned Italian bread crumbs do.)

Remove the chicken from the oven, sprinkle with additional grated cheese, and let it sit briefly before serving with fresh parsley and lemon wedges.

Skinless, boneless poached chicken breast is a great starting point for fast entrée salads, casseroles, and sandwiches. Eat this plain poached chicken while it is still warm with a sauce of your choosing—cranberry sauce, various chutneys, bottled lingonberries, and Quick Cumberland Sauce (page 152) are the favorites in my home—or else chill the chicken for slicing, cubing, or shredding later.

SERVES 4

NONSTICK COOKING SPRAY

4 SKINLESS, BONELESS CHICKEN BREAST HALVES (ABOUT 1^1/$_2$ POUNDS)

JUICE OF 1 LEMON

PREHEAT YOUR TOASTER OVEN to 400 degrees F. Spray an 8 × 8-inch or 9 × 9-inch baking dish with nonstick cooking spray.

Wash the chicken under cold running water and pat it dry with paper towels. Trim away any fat. Place the chicken in the baking dish; it will fit snugly. Sprinkle the lemon juice over the surface of the chicken and cover the dish securely with tinfoil, pressing the foil down on the surface of the chicken. Bake for 25 minutes, or until the chicken is white and firm to the touch. Remove and serve, or let cool before transferring to a storage container and refrigerating for later use.

*This recipe brings you saltimbocca (sort of) adapted
for an economical cut of chicken and the tidiness of toaster-oven
roasting. Serve with rice or crusty bread.*

SERVES 2 OR 3

NONSTICK COOKING SPRAY, BUTTER, OR OIL

6 SKINLESS, BONELESS CHICKEN THIGHS (ABOUT 1 POUND)

FRESHLY GROUND BLACK PEPPER

SIX $^1/_2$-INCH-THICK STICKS OF SWISS GRUYÈRE CHEESE

3 SLICES AIR-CURED SALTED HAM (SERRANO OR PROSCIUTTO), CUT IN HALF, OR AN
    EQUIVALENT AMOUNT OF COUNTRY HAM

3 SAGE LEAVES, HALVED (OPTIONAL)

SALT

$^1/_3$ CUP FRESHLY GRATED PARMESAN CHEESE

$^1/_3$ CUP DRIED SEASONED BREAD CRUMBS OR CRACKER MEAL

2 TABLESPOONS UNSALTED BUTTER, CUT INTO 6 PATS

PREHEAT YOUR TOASTER OVEN to 350 degrees F. Spray, butter, or oil a baking dish large enough to hold the thighs snugly.

Wash the thighs in cool water and pat them dry with paper towels. Lay each thigh flat on a cutting board, sprinkle with pepper, and put a stick of cheese, half a slice of ham, and half of a sage leaf if using into the center of each thigh. Roll the thigh meat around the filling. Place these little parcels, seam side down, in the baking dish. Sprinkle the tops with salt, pepper, Parmesan, and bread crumbs, and top each one with a pat of butter.

Bake for 25 to 30 minutes, switching the toaster oven to broil for the last few minutes if desired to brown the tops.

I have always equated piecrust (even premade crust) with trouble, *so I was delighted to come across this "quiche," which has no crust at all. Guests hardly seem to notice. The only trick here is to heat the pie plate in the oven after spraying it with nonstick spray but before adding the egg mixture. Since this quiche is best eaten warm, reheat leftovers at low heat in your toaster oven or microwave.*

SERVES 4

NONSTICK COOKING SPRAY

6 LARGE EGGS

$^1/_4$ CUP HEAVY CREAM

ABOUT $^1/_4$ TEASPOON FRESHLY GROUND BLACK PEPPER

$^1/_8$ TEASPOON FRESHLY GRATED NUTMEG (OPTIONAL)

1 CUP CHOPPED HAM (ABOUT 6 OUNCES)

1 CUP SHREDDED SHARP CHEDDAR CHEESE (4 OUNCES)

2 TABLESPOONS CHOPPED CHIVES (OPTIONAL)

3 SHALLOTS, FINELY CHOPPED AND EITHER SAUTÉED OR MICROWAVED IN 2 TABLESPOONS
UNSALTED BUTTER UNTIL TRANSLUCENT (OPTIONAL)

$^1/_4$ CUP SHREDDED CHEESE FOR TOPPING (PREFERABLY FRESHLY GRATED PARMESAN OR
SWISS GRUYÈRE, BUT MORE CHEDDAR WILL ALSO DO FINE)

PREHEAT YOUR (TOASTER) OVEN to 400 degrees F.

Spray a 9-inch glass pie plate with nonstick cooking spray and put it in the oven.

Beat the eggs in a 1-quart measuring cup. Stir in the cream, pepper to taste, nutmeg if desired, ham, Cheddar, and chives and shallots if using. Pour the mixture into the heated pie dish. Bake for 20 minutes, until puffed and set in the center. Remove to a cooling rack and sprinkle with the topping cheese. Let stand until the cheese is melted, about 10 minutes, before serving.

Cheese Grating Tip: Commercially prepared grated cheese such as Jack or Cheddar costs only pennies more than a bar of the same and is a great time-saver. But should you choose to grate your own on an as needed basis, spray the surface of the grater lightly with nonstick cooking spray and the process will go much faster, with easier cleanup as well.

If you are going to go to the trouble of making a real quiche, you are probably doing so for guests, and thus you don't want the quiche to look as if you bought it. Using your own glass pie plate (that is, not using a prepared frozen crust in an aluminum pan) and creating a few irregularities in the packaged, premade crust will be enough to convince most people that you have labored long and hard to give them pleasure. Glass pie dishes have other benefits: They help make the crust flaky and dry, and they double as a serving (and storage) dish. Take the extra steps outlined below for an optimally flaky, dry crust.

SERVES 4

1 REFRIGERATED, FOLDED (OR, EVEN BETTER, "UNROLL AND BAKE") PIECRUST

6 SHALLOTS, FINELY CHOPPED

4 TABLESPOONS UNSALTED BUTTER

1 CUP HEAVY CREAM

$1/2$ TEASPOON SALT

$1/4$ TEASPOON FRESHLY GRATED NUTMEG

4 LARGE EGGS, BEATEN

1 TABLESPOON DIJON MUSTARD

$1 1/4$ CUPS GRATED SWISS GRUYÈRE CHEESE (ABOUT 5 OUNCES)

$1/2$ CUP FINELY CHOPPED COUNTRY HAM (ABOUT 3 OUNCES; YOU CAN SUBSTITUTE
    CHOPPED SERRANO HAM, PROSCIUTTO, OR COOKED, CRUMBLED BACON)

PREHEAT YOUR (TOASTER) OVEN to 400 degrees F.

Let the refrigerated crust come to room temperature before you attempt to unfold it. It will probably crack anyway. (The new "unroll and bake" piecrusts work better than the folded ones.) Fit the crust into the 9-inch glass pie plate, patching up any tears, and crimping or fussing with the edges as you like. Then put the pie plate in the freezer for at least 15 minutes to chill—30 minutes if possible.

Meanwhile, cook the shallots in the butter in a large nonstick saucepan until translucent (or microwave the shallots and butter together for 1 to 2 minutes to achieve the same result). Put the shallot-butter mixture in a bowl, then add the cream, salt, nutmeg, and beaten eggs, and stir together until mixed.

When the crust is well chilled, prick the bottom of it with a fork, then smear it with the Dijon mustard and sprinkle on a couple of tablespoons of the cheese. Place the crust in the oven for 10 minutes, then remove it and reduce the temperature to 325 degrees F. If the crust has bubbled up at all, press it back into place gently with a fork. Scatter the ham over the bottom of the crust and distribute the remaining cheese on top of it.

Pour the egg mixture over the ham and cheese and return the dish to the oven. Bake for 35 to 40 minutes, until puffed and set in the center. Remove and let it cool on a rack for 10 minutes before serving.

Itty Bitty Pasta: Shortcut Central

PASTA AND PREPARED PASTA SAUCES are old standbys of the small kitchen, since both have an almost indefinite shelf life. But often the idea of boiling up a big pot of water on a small stove, dealing with the steamy mess of hefting all that boiling water into a small, crowded sink in close and poorly ventilated quarters, and then facing the added challenge of saucing your pasta without spattering yourself or dirtying a big bulky pasta bowl (which you also have no place to store) can defeat the space-challenged cook before he or she even begins.

But really good, quick, easy pasta is possible in small kitchens if you consider the following sneaky tricks.

1. No huge pot of water. The only reason to boil a big pot of water in a small kitchen is if you have long pasta that won't fit in a smaller pot. So . . . cook short pasta instead! Half a pound of pasta will feed two; only 3 quarts of water are officially recommended by pasta manufacturers for this amount of pasta, but short pasta can cook in less water. You can get by with using the water in a 2-quart saucepan (and I've had perfectly satisfactory results using a 1-quart saucepan); just stir the boiling pasta a little more to keep it from clumping. You have broken the rules here, true—but the pasta police are not going to come and arrest you.

2. Pick the right dried pasta. The finest dried pastas are made with durum semolina, a wheat that requires more work to turn into pasta but that yields better flavor, texture, and color. It is firm and never mushy, with real presence in a finished dish. The best semolina pastas tend to be Italian and cost about 20 cents more per pound; De Cecco is the most famous brand.

3. Use a self-straining nonstick saucepan with a lock-on lid to cook your pasta. That way there's no need to use a colander or to clear the sink. Once the pasta has been drained, return the saucepan to the stove, remove the lid, add the sauce (which will usually have cooked up quite well in an omelet pan), and cook the pasta and sauce together briefly to finish the dish. Then plate it up right there in the  kitchen. Because the interior of your pot is nonstick, even the cheesiest pasta sauce will wash up with no problem, and this way there is no serving bowl to scrub up afterward.

4. Make an easy, interesting sauce. Many Italian sauces for pasta come together in the time it takes to boil water. So don't reach

for a jar of something that tastes like it comes from a jar (unless of course that's what you like). And whatever your choice of sauce, don't drown the pasta in it—too much sauce makes even good pasta soggy.

5. Dare to turn your pasta into a one-course meal. Italian cooking usually separates the pasta from the main course, but if you are cooking informally, just add a little more meat, chicken, vegetables, or fish to the pasta and sauce, using some of the ways suggested in the following recipes as inspiration—or, if you like your pasta simple, consider having a traditional antipasto of sliced meats, cheeses, and vegetables to start off your meal.

Now that you've got the basic strategy down, here are some classic easy sauces.

*If you omit the sage in this recipe, the dish becomes every kid's
favorite, spaghetti with butter and Parmesan—a very comforting
dish for a quiet night in. But fresh sage (that is, not dried)
transforms it into something more "adult."
Fettuccine is the traditional pasta choice, but you can use penne
if you aren't interested in cooking a long pasta.*

SERVES 2

$^1/_2$ POUND DRIED PASTA OF CHOICE

4 TABLESPOONS ($^1/_2$ STICK) UNSALTED BUTTER

1 GARLIC CLOVE, PEELED AND SPLIT IN HALF

6 TO 10 LARGE FRESH SAGE LEAVES, WASHED, DRIED, AND CHOPPED
   INTO FINE RIBBONS

SEA SALT

FRESHLY GROUND BLACK PEPPER

FRESHLY GRATED PARMESAN CHEESE

PUT THE PASTA WATER ON TO BOIL, salting it a little more heavily than
usual. When it boils, add the pasta and time the cooking according
to package directions.

Melt the butter in an omelet pan over moderate heat. Add the garlic
and sage and cook gently; do not let the butter brown or burn. Add
a pinch or two of salt and pepper.   *(continued)*

Remove the garlic and discard. Then add 2 tablespoons of the boiling pasta water as the pasta cooks and keep the sauce warm.

Drain the pasta, add the sauce, and toss to coat, adding a substantial amount of Parmesan as you do so. Serve with additional Parmesan.

VARIATION: ONE-DISH MEAL Add $^{1}/_{2}$ cup chopped cooked chicken or turkey and $^{1}/_{2}$ cup chopped cooked spinach and adjust seasonings.

A great, fast late-night meal. Many people fear and despise the tiny anchovy yet will enjoy the savory taste of foods prepared with anchovies so long as the fish themselves are not recognizably present. *Sneak them into this sauce (they pretty much disappear) and you may be surprised by the reception.*
Linguine is traditional here, but if you want to use a short pasta, try conchiglie or penne rigati.

SERVES 2

^{1}/2 POUND DRIED PASTA OF CHOICE

4 TABLESPOONS GOOD-QUALITY OLIVE OIL

3 GARLIC CLOVES, THINLY SLICED

HALF A 2-OUNCE CAN ANCHOVIES IN OLIVE OIL (OPTIONAL BUT VERY GOOD)

RED PEPPER FLAKES

FINELY CHOPPED FRESH PARSLEY TO TASTE (ALSO OPTIONAL BUT GOOD)

2 TABLESPOONS DRIED BREAD CRUMBS OR CRACKER MEAL (TOASTED GENTLY IN A
    NONSTICK PAN OR IN THE TOASTER OVEN IF YOU HAVE A MOMENT)

PUT THE PASTA WATER ON TO BOIL. When it boils, add the pasta and time the cooking according to package directions.

Heat the olive oil in an omelet pan, and cook the garlic slices until they are light golden. Then add the anchovies if using, along with half the olive oil in the can. Cook the mixture gently until the anchovies fall apart. If the garlic gets too brown, remove it (but if you cook it gently, you won't have to, and the sauce tastes much better if you leave it in). Finally, add $^1/_4$ cup of the water from the boiling pasta. Keep the sauce warm until the pasta is done. Drain the pasta, then toss it in the pasta pot with the sauce to coat, sprinkling on the red pepper flakes and parsley as desired. Just before serving, sprinkle each portion with the toasted bread crumbs and drizzle with a little more fine olive oil.

NOTE: If you omit the anchovy from the recipe, toss the garlic-oil pasta with $^1/_2$ cup freshly grated Pecorino Romano cheese (about 2 ounces) as well as the bread crumbs.

VARIATION: ONE-DISH MEAL Warm 6 to 8 medium cooked shrimp in the sauce. If you have raw shrimp, peel them and add them to the sauce at the same time you add the anchovies and cook until firm and opaque (don't worry about deveining the shrimp unless you are fussy or trying to impress someone). If you are using cooked, frozen salad shrimp, add 1 cup of them to the sauce when you add the water from the boiling pasta, and heat until warmed through. (Note: If adding shrimp, do not add cheese.)

SAUSAGE AND BROCCOLI RABE WITH PASTA

This is a nicely balanced combination of pork and bitter greens that tastes great with short pasta. Kale works well as a substitute for broccoli rabe (and is very good for you too!), but if you have space problems in your refrigerator, go with broccoli rabe—it's denser and requires less room. Frozen broccoli rabe or kale, more compact but less fresh, also works just fine.

SERVES 2

$^1/_2$ POUND DRIED PASTA OF CHOICE (ORECCHIETTE IS VERY GOOD HERE)

4 ITALIAN SAUSAGES (ABOUT 1 POUND)

3 TABLESPOONS OLIVE OIL

2 GARLIC CLOVES, PEELED AND CUT IN HALF

$^1/_2$ BUNCH BROCCOLI RABE (ABOUT $^1/_2$ POUND), CHOPPED

SALT

$^1/_4$ CUP LOW-SODIUM CHICKEN BROTH

RED PEPPER FLAKES

FRESHLY GRATED PARMESAN OR PECORINO CHEESE

PUT THE PASTA WATER ON TO BOIL. When it boils, add the pasta and time the cooking according to package directions.

Squeeze or cut the sausage out of its casing and fry it in a nonstick sauté pan until cooked, breaking it up as you go. Remove the sausage meat to a bowl and drain off all but a tablespoon of the fat. Add the olive oil to the sauté pan and, when the oil is hot, add the garlic. Cook until the garlic is golden brown, then remove and discard it and add the broccoli rabe.

Sauté the broccoli rabe over high heat, adding salt to taste. Add the chicken broth and sausage, cover, and cook down until the broccoli rabe is wilted. Add red pepper flakes to taste. When the pasta is done, drain it and then add to the sauté pan, tossing to mix. Add more olive oil as needed. Serve with grated Parmesan or, for a sharper taste, grated pecorino.

VARIATION: ONE-DISH MEAL If you require more meat in your diet, just add a couple of additional sausages.

Cold Plates and Composed Dinner Salads: or, Cook's Night Off

SOMETIMES THE BEST COOKING IS NO COOKING AT ALL, particularly if you had a big lunch, a long day at work, or just came home feeling cranky. Instead of struggling with your *&$#$! IBK, declare a holiday from cooking and instead put together a plate of delectable small things out of the fridge. A couple of slices of toast or a mug of soup can add warmth on a cold night. Here are some suggestions for good foods to keep on hand.

Cold Plates

Antipasto Plate—assorted Italian cold cuts (try mortadella, capicolla, Genoa salami, abruzzese dry salami, soppressata), a piece of young pecorino cheese, bocconcini (little balls of marinated mozzarella), bread sticks, olives, marinated artichoke hearts, a small hunk of fresh Parmesan cheese, roasted red peppers, marinated mushrooms

Charcuterie Plate—country pâté, rosette de Lyon salami, picholine olives, cornichons, jambon de Bayonne (or prosciutto or Serrano ham), boiled ham, vinaigrette potato salad, grainy or Dijon mustard, crusty French bread

Cold Chicken Plate—sliced Poached Chicken Breast (page 121), cranberry sauce, A Week of Mayonnaise (page 149) or Quick Cumberland Sauce (page 152), lettuce, potato salad, sliced hard-boiled egg, toasted and buttered whole wheat bread, broccoli sprouts

German Cold Cut Plate—liverwurst, Westphalian ham, beef cervelat salami, German bologna, cold Roast Boneless Center-Cut Loin of Pork (page 112), various German mustards, heavy rye or pumpernickel, pickles, Real German Coleslaw (page 168)

Herring Plate—herring in wine sauce, herring in cream sauce, herring in mustard sauce, rollmops, brown bread or limpa (a Swedish bread flavored with molasses and caraway), Wilted Cucumber Salad (page 170), Akvavit or vodka and/or beer. (When ambitious, peel and boil a potato—see page 161—as an accompaniment.)

Meat Loaf Plate—plain meat loaf at room temperature (or pâté), Quick Cumberland Sauce (page 152), cranberry sauce or lingonberries, Wilted Cucumber Salad (page 170), buttered rye toast

Middle Eastern Plate—tabbouleh, hummus, baba ganoush, taramasalata, warmed pita bread, carrot sticks, olives, stuffed grape leaves, extra virgin olive oil, yogurt, feta cheese

Plowman's Lunch Plate—Stilton cheese, celery sticks, carrot sticks, chutney or Branston pickle (a sweet and savory brown relish made of assorted vegetables and dates, available at food specialty stores or www.ukgoods.com), pickled onions, brown bread and unsalted butter

Shrimp Cocktail Plate—cooked jumbo shrimp, cocktail sauce, shredded iceberg lettuce, lemon, crudités, dinner rolls and unsalted butter

Smoked Salmon Plate—buttered brown bread, smoked salmon, lemon, fresh dill, Wilted Cucumber Salad (page 170) or mesclun salad

Composed Dinner Salads

Composed salads are essentially cold dinners served on a bed of lettuce—they are that easy and that versatile.

NIÇOISE SALAD

A quick trip to the Côte d'Azur. If you like, you can boil the egg in the same lightly salted water as the potatoes: just start the egg in cold water, and when the water reaches a boil, add the potatoes. Remove the egg seven minutes after the water boils and run it under cold water. The potatoes will be done thirteen minutes later—twenty minutes in all—which is just about how long it takes to assemble everything else. Serve with crusty bread.

SERVES 1

ONE 6-OUNCE CAN TUNA IN OLIVE OIL

1 TABLESPOON CAPERS

6 GOOD-QUALITY OLIVES, PREFERABLY NIÇOISE OR PICHOLINE

$^1/_2$ CUP LIGHTLY COOKED GREEN BEANS OR HARICOTS VERTS

1 HARD-BOILED EGG, SLICED IN HALF, TOPPED WITH AN ANCHOVY IF DESIRED

2 TO 3 FRESHLY BOILED NEW POTATOES (PAGE 161), SLICED OR HALVED

ANCHOVIES (OPTIONAL)

A FEW LEAVES OF BOSTON, RED LEAF, OR GREEN LEAF LETTUCE

EXTRA VIRGIN OLIVE OIL

JUICE OF $^1/_2$ LEMON

SALT

FRESHLY GROUND BLACK PEPPER

ARRANGE THE TUNA, capers, olives, green beans, hard-boiled egg, potatoes and anchovies if using, on a few leaves of lettuce in a shallow bowl or on a platter, drizzling on olive oil to taste and the lemon juice. Season with salt and pepper to taste, and feel free to add additional anchovies if desired.

TUNA AND WHITE BEAN "EMERGENCY" SALAD

This quick, hearty main course salad is made up of things that store almost indefinitely in your cupboard and refrigerator, so it is a great "emergency" dinner. It keeps very well in the refrigerator but should always be brought to room temperature before serving.
This salad goes beautifully with crusty bread, Croutons (page 87), or toast. If you are in the midst of a true *pantry emergency (meaning you haven't even got bread), it also goes well with saltines or other crackers.*

SERVES 4

ONE 7-OUNCE CAN TUNA IN OLIVE OIL

ONE 15-OUNCE CAN CANNELLINI BEANS

1 LARGE SHALLOT, FINELY CHOPPED

SALT

FRESHLY GROUND BLACK PEPPER

JUICE OF $^1/_2$ LEMON

ABOUT $^1/_2$ CUP BEST-QUALITY EXTRA VIRGIN OLIVE OIL

FINELY CHOPPED FRESH PARSLEY

(continued)

Open the tuna and transfer the contents of the can, including the olive oil, to a bowl. Flake apart the tuna until no large chunks remain. Drain the cannellini beans and rinse them thoroughly in a sieve under cold running water. Drain off the water and add the beans to the tuna. Place the shallot in the sieve and pour 2 cups of boiling water over it. Drain it and add it to the bowl. Mix the salad gently and season to taste with salt, pepper, freshly squeezed lemon juice, and a little more olive oil than you might think absolutely necessary.

Top each portion with finely chopped fresh parsley at serving time.

BACON LOVER'S SPINACH SALAD

This is a very substantial starter for two people, but it can also be served as a main course dinner salad. Cleaned spinach is available by the bag; with a hard-boiled egg, good croutons, and a whole lotta bacon, it's also a very fast and filling meal. (If you are using fresh, unpackaged spinach, wash it very carefully to get rid of any sand.)

SERVES 2

6 SLICES THICKLY CUT BACON (ABOUT 10 OUNCES)

1 SMALL SHALLOT, CHOPPED

1 TEASPOON SUGAR

$^1/_4$ CUP CIDER VINEGAR

SALT

FRESHLY GROUND BLACK PEPPER

ONE 10-OUNCE BAG SPINACH GREENS, FRESHLY WASHED AND DRIED

2 HARD-BOILED EGGS, SLICED INTO HALVES OR QUARTERS

5 CHERRY TOMATOES CUT IN HALF

1 BATCH OF CROUTONS (PAGE 87), OR 4 BREAD CROUTONS (SEE NOTE)

FRY THE BACON; remove it and drain on a paper towel. When cool, break into bite-sized pieces.

To make the dressing, drain off all but 2 tablespoons of bacon drippings and sauté the shallot in it. Add the sugar, cider vinegar, salt, and pepper, and heat to boiling. Meanwhile place the spinach in a bowl. Pour the dressing over it, toss, and garnish with the egg slices, bacon, and croutons.

NOTE: To make bread croutons, rub 4 slices crusty bread with olive oil, sprinkle with salt, and bake in your toaster oven at 400 degrees F until golden brown

Although fish is a wonderfully healthful food, many people with small kitchens balk at the idea of cooking it, mostly out of concern for the strong and lingering odors it can generate—one incinerated mackerel in a small apartment being enough to last most of us a lifetime. My own experiments with fish (which began when my sister, Margaret, caught and shipped me a 25-pound wild salmon from Alaska, beautifully portioned out and shrink-wrapped) have taught me that sometimes fresh fish of the nonoily sort can be cooked and enjoyed in small spaces with spectacular (and tidy) results.

Wild salmon is entirely different in taste and texture from farmed salmon: It is lean, meaty, and deep orange when cooked—so if you have a choice, choose wild. If your salmon fillet happens to be deep-frozen, place it (tightly wrapped in waterproof plastic) under cold running water until it is just defrosted, about 4 minutes.

SERVES 2

2 CENTER-CUT WILD SALMON FILLETS (7 TO 9 OUNCES EACH), WITH A UNIFORM
    THICKNESS OF $1^1/4$ INCHES

2 TEASPOONS OLIVE OIL OR UNSALTED BUTTER, MELTED

SALT

FRESHLY GROUND BLACK PEPPER

FINELY CHOPPED FRESH PARSLEY

LEMON WEDGES

PREHEAT YOUR TOASTER OVEN to 400 degrees F. Place the dish in which you are going to bake the fish in the toaster oven.

Rub the salmon fillets with the oil or melted butter and place them in the heated baking dish skin side down. Season with salt and pepper. Bake the fish for 10 minutes, then remove the fish from the oven (checking with your instant-read thermometer that it has cooked to an internal temperature of 125 degrees F) and let it sit for 3 minutes in the hot dish (where it will continue to cook) before putting it on your plate. Serve with additional melted butter, fresh parsley, and lemon wedges.

SHRIMP SCAMPI

Shrimp is popular even with those (such as children) who are picky about seafood. Shrimp stores quite compactly in the freezer, so it is a good food choice for the itty bitty kitchen. Shell-on frozen shrimp have much more flavor than do shrimp that have been cooked and peeled prior to freezing. The quickest way I know to prepare shrimp is simply to boil it with a little water, vinegar, and commercially prepared Old Bay seasoning, following the instructions on the seasoning box. But Shrimp Scampi, the classic Italian American preparation, is easy and versatile. It can be eaten over rice, over linguini, or simply from individual gratin dishes accompanied by good crusty bread to soak up the buttery, garlicky sauce.

SERVES 2

4 TABLESPOONS ($^1/_2$ STICK) UNSALTED BUTTER

$^1/_4$ CUP OLIVE OIL

1 $^1/_2$ TO 2 POUNDS PEELED, DEVEINED SHRIMP (PREFERABLY WILD GULF WHITE OR GULF PINK SHRIMP, AS LARGE AS YOU CAN AFFORD)

2 GARLIC CLOVES, FINELY CHOPPED

JUICE OF 1 LEMON

SEA SALT

FINELY CHOPPED FRESH PARSLEY

FRESH BREAD CRUMBS

LEMON WEDGES

HEAT THE BUTTER AND OLIVE OIL together in a sauté pan. When the foam from the butter subsides, add the shrimp and the garlic at the same time, cooking until the shrimp are opaque, about 3 minutes. Remove from heat, add the lemon juice and salt to taste, toss, sprinkle with fresh parsley and bread crumbs, and serve with lemon wedges.

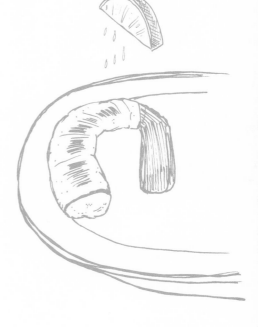

While commercially prepared sauces such as ketchup, mustard, applesauce,

and chutney are all very useful, a good homemade sauce (particularly one

that keeps well) makes simple food seem much more interesting.

Here are three personal favorites.

If you have a case of the blahs and are not feeling inspired to cook, just make a quick batch of homemade mayonnaise and use it in salads and sandwiches, on hard-boiled eggs, as a dip for crisp-tender cooked vegetables, or even as a sauce on warm cooked foods such as baked salmon or poached chicken breasts. (It will also do amazing things to a bag of quick-thawed salad shrimp and a halved ripe avocado.) This big batch of blender mayonnaise will last two people about a week—after which you (and your waistline) will probably be ready to go back to a non-mayonnaise lifestyle. If keeping this much homemade mayo in the house seems like too much of a temptation, just halve the recipe.

Note: It's best not to use olive oil in this recipe because its flavor is too strong.

MAKES ABOUT 1 ^{1}/$_2$ CUPS

2 LARGE EGG YOLKS, AT ROOM TEMPERATURE

2 HEAPING TEASPOONS DIJON MUSTARD

^{1}/$_2$ TEASPOON SALT

1 ^{1}/$_2$ CUPS PEANUT OR SAFFLOWER OIL

JUICE OF 1 LEMON

FINELY GROUND BLACK PEPPER

CAYENNE PEPPER

IN A BLENDER, mix the egg yolks, mustard, and salt at low speed. Very, very slowly (particularly at the beginning) add the oil in a thin stream. When all the oil has been incorporated, add the lemon juice and seasonings to taste. Taste and correct the seasonings to suit yourself.

NOTE: The egg yolks need to be at room temperature before you begin. Run the eggs under warm water for a while if you are impatient. Cold eggs don't work well, and can result in a "broken" mayonnaise (aka a big, gloppy mess). Also, sniff your oil just to be double sure it is not stale or rancid. If your mayonnaise separates ("breaks"), remove it from the blender, place an additional egg yolk (at room temperature) into the blender, and add the juice of half a lemon. Blend thoroughly, then add the broken mayonnaise to the egg yolk and lemon juice mixture a little at a time while the blender is running. All will come right.

For fastest cleanup, see the Blender Cleanup Tip on page 83.

VARIATION: CURRIED MAYONNAISE Add 1 teaspoon good fresh curry powder to 1 cup of the mayonnaise, or more if you like a strong curry taste.

While chateaubriand (page 101) is a very tender and trouble-free cut of beef, it is also very mild in flavor—and benefits decisively from an accompanying sauce such as béarnaise. This recipe will yield more than you need for the beef alone, but it goes well with asparagus too, and leftovers make a great sandwich spread or topping for hard-boiled eggs. Since béarnaise is good with any roast meat or fish, don't feel you must make chateaubriand in order to eat it!

Make sure your egg yolks are at room temperature, since cold yolks cannot absorb butter well. You can move them in that direction by putting the eggs under warm running water for several minutes.

MAKES ABOUT 2 $^1/_2$ CUPS

$^1/_2$ CUP TARRAGON VINEGAR

$^1/_2$ CUP DRY WHITE WINE OR VERMOUTH

2 TABLESPOONS MINCED SHALLOTS OR SCALLIONS

1 TEASPOON DRIED TARRAGON

$^1/_2$ TEASPOON SALT

$^1/_4$ TEASPOON FRESHLY GROUND BLACK PEPPER

6 LARGE EGG YOLKS, AT ROOM TEMPERATURE

1 $^1/_4$ CUPS (2 $^1/_2$ STICKS) UNSALTED BUTTER, MELTED BUT NOT TOO HOT

BOIL THE VINEGAR, wine, shallots, tarragon, salt, and pepper in a small saucepan until the liquid is reduced to 4 tablespoons. Let it cool. Place the egg yolks and the reduced liquid in the container of your blender. Blend at high speed for 30 seconds and then begin to add the melted butter a little at a time. Do this as slowly as you can. Should your béarnaise separate, empty it out of the blender, wash out the blender, add an egg yolk at room temperature, blend, and feed the separated sauce back into the blender again, drop by drop.

For fastest cleanup, see the Blender Cleanup Tip on page 83.

For fastest cleanup, see the Blender Cleanup Tip on page 83.

QUICK CUMBERLAND SAUCE

Quick Cumberland Sauce can cause a sensation at your table—a good thing when you are sneakily serving guests prepared foods like pâté, or otherwise boring fare, like turkey breast. This recipe makes a thin, tart, liquid sauce, so it is substantially different from that sugary jellied version of Cumberland sauce that is sometimes available by the jar (and at a price) from specialty markets. Quick Cumberland Sauce tastes great with Skillet Ham Slice (page 105), cold roast turkey, leftover meat loaf (page 96), or any rich and gamey pâté or terrine. It is also good with poached chicken breast (page 121).
This recipe is easily doubled—and doubling it may be a good idea, since the sauce will last up to 3 weeks in the refrigerator. Incidentally, leftover port wine lasts almost indefinitely and pairs beautifully with dark chocolate. With the possible addition of an orange, the two make a fast, easy, and interesting no-work dessert.

MAKES ABOUT $^3/_4$ CUP

1 SMALL LEMON

1 LARGE NAVEL ORANGE

$^1/_4$ CUP GOOD-QUALITY RED CURRANT JELLY

$^1/_4$ CUP RUBY PORT

1 TEASPOON DRY MUSTARD

1 TEASPOON GROUND GINGER

HEAT 1 TO 1 $^1/_2$ CUPS WATER to a boil in a small saucepan. Wash the lemon and orange. Use a sharp knife or vegetable peeler to remove their zest in large strips. Set the lemon and orange aside. Cut the zest into very fine, thin strips. Trim the strips so they are about $^1/_2$ inch long or less. Place the strips of zest in boiling water for 5 minutes and then drain them and blot them dry on paper towels. Wash out the saucepan to get rid of any remaining bitter oils.

Place the red currant jelly and port together in the cleaned saucepan and cook them over low heat for 5 to 10 minutes, until the jelly is melted, whisking if necessary.

In a small bowl or large measuring cup, mix the mustard and ginger together with the juice of half the lemon. Pour it into the saucepan of port-jelly mixture, along with the juice of the orange and the strips of zest, and mix well. Pour into a jar, cover, and chill thoroughly before serving.

Sure, you can eat just one thing for dinner (what person has not had a brief but memorable encounter with a pork chop?). But your food will feel more like a meal if you have something else on the plate. When confronted with a choice of sides, my first inclination is almost invariably for a starch—but salads are so easy and good that having both starch *and* salad is hardly out of the question.

Starches

A GOOD (STARCHY) SIDE DISH is often enough to make a simple dinner memorable—and a double-starch meal (one featuring both potatoes and stuffing, for example) is nearly always a crowd-pleaser. So here are some of the easiest and most satisfying.

BAKED POTATO (VIA TOASTER OVEN, MICROWAVE, OR BOTH)

The microwave will "bake" a potato for you in 4 to 8 minutes (and is so frequently called upon to do so that many models now feature a special potato button), but the result is usually a sodden excuse for the real deal. A good baked potato has a roasty-toasty character, with a sturdy, crusty skin and dry-fluffy interior.

Idahos or russets make the best baked potatoes; scrub them, prick them all over with a fork, rub them lightly with oil, and put them in the toaster oven for 1 hour at 450 degrees F or $1^{1}/2$ hours at 350 degrees F. If you want a quicker potato, pierce the potato, oil it, microwave it according to your machine's instructions (8 minutes on high is probably more than enough), then put it in the toaster oven for 15 minutes at 450 degrees F. You'll get a much better, crispy-toasty result.

(continued)

VARIATION: BAKED POTATO WEDGE "FRIES" Preheat your (toaster) oven to 400 degrees F. Scrub a baking potato and cut it into 8 wedges. Dry the wedges with a towel and rub them with olive oil. Add salt to taste (or seasoned salt). Place the wedges in an ovenproof dish (lined with aluminum foil for easiest cleanup) and roast for 45 minutes, shaking and turning the potatoes once or twice for even browning. The wedges will be brown and crispy and very much like a French fry if eaten right away.

BAKED SWEET POTATO Sweet potatoes cook in slightly less time than regular potatoes, in both a microwave and a toaster oven. They don't suffer quite as much from microwaving, but still benefit from cooking for 5 minutes in the microwave, and 15 minutes in the oven. Don't bother oiling or piercing them, though. In a toaster oven, they will cook in only 35 minutes at 425 degrees F. A piece of foil beneath them in the toaster oven will catch any sugary drips. Six minutes on high in a microwave will be enough for a medium sweet potato; 8 minutes for a larger one.

Ham, cheese, and shallot are a very dependable flavor combination, but feel free to experiment. In England, "jacket" potatoes are routinely stuffed with just about anything you can imagine, including tuna, sweet corn, and chutney. Fridge-friendly ingredients like salsa, avocado, and dried or cooked sausage are probably more to the American taste. Sour cream is great, but yogurt works surprisingly well, too.

SERVES 1

BAKE A POTATO (PAGE 155), then split it open. Scoop out the interior and mash it up in a small bowl; add unsalted butter; grated sharp Cheddar, Gruyère, and/or Parmesan cheese to taste; a beaten egg; some chopped ham; some chopped shallot or scallion if you like; salt and freshly ground black pepper; and maybe even a little nutmeg. Stuff this mixture back into the potato skin and top with additional grated cheese. Return it to the (toaster) oven at 450 degrees F for 10 minutes. Run it under the broiler for the last few minutes to brown it if you like.

"COUCH POTATO" STUFFED BAKED POTATO

This is probably the easiest, laziest dinner ever. Just make sure to use real Italian sweet Gorgonzola, which comes in soft, buttery slabs; the crumbled, acrid, domestically produced salad cheese known as Gorgonzola (or "Gorg") really won't do the job.

SERVES 1

BAKE A POTATO (PAGE 155). Split it open, mash the interior, and top with equal parts unsalted butter and sweet Gorgonzola cheese (in a quantity befitting your appetite) with salt and freshly ground black pepper to taste. If you are being *supremely* lazy, fresh parsley and/or chives are optional.

POTATO GRATIN

When you are eating simple roasted meats or poultry, this is an accompanying potato dish with richness and subtlety. Potatoes simmered in milk or cream create their own sauce all by themselves; topped with some grated cheese they become even more interesting. Baked in individual gratin dishes with chopped ham and sprinkled more heavily with cheese, they become a quick and delicious meal in themselves, perfect for a cold winter evening.

Decide how many potatoes you need; generally 1 large potato per person is enough.

SERVES 1

NONSTICK COOKING SPRAY

1 LARGE POTATO (RUSSET OR IDAHO WORKS BEST)

ABOUT $3/4$ CUP MILK, CREAM, OR A COMBINATION OF BOTH

SALT

FRESHLY GROUND BLACK PEPPER

$1/2$ GARLIC CLOVE, FINELY CHOPPED

PINCH OF CAYENNE PEPPER

$1/2$ BAY LEAF (OPTIONAL)

PINCH OF DRIED THYME

PINCH OF FRESHLY GRATED NUTMEG

1 TABLESPOON UNSALTED BUTTER

$1/4$ CUP GRATED GRUYÈRE OR PARMESAN CHEESE (ABOUT 1 OUNCE)

$1/4$ CUP CHOPPED COUNTRY HAM OR REGULAR HAM (ABOUT 3 OUNCES)

PREHEAT YOUR (TOASTER) OVEN to 350 degrees F. Spray an individual gratin dish with nonstick cooking spray to ensure easy cleanup. (Use an 8 × 8-inch dish or a 9-inch pie dish for 3 to 4 potatoes.)

Peel the potato and slice it into disks; place it in a saucepan with milk or cream nearly to cover, adding the butter, salt and pepper to taste (being careful with the salt if you are going to add ham), the garlic, cayenne, bay leaf if using, thyme, and nutmeg.

Bring this mixture to a boil, then lower the heat and simmer for about 5 minutes.

Remove the pot from the heat, and spoon the mixture into the prepared baking dish. At this point, remove the bay leaf if you added one. Top the potato mixture with the ham and a thin layer of grated cheese and bake for about 50 minutes, or until the potato slices are easily pierced with a fork. (If you like, you can cover the dish with foil for the first 30 minutes of cooking for a more delicate crust.) Cooking times will vary according to the size of the dish you are using and the depth of the potatoes in the dish.

Potatoes of different sorts need to be treated in different ways. To boil regular potatoes, peel and quarter them, add cold water to cover, and 1 tablespoon of salt per pound of potatoes. Bring to a gentle boil, then reduce the heat and simmer for 20 minutes, until the potatoes are easily pierced with a knife. Drain them, then let them sit in the pot for a minute or so with a very gentle heat underneath them to help them dry out. Boiled new potatoes (also known as baby creamers, and available in red, white, and Yukon gold varieties) must be added to an ample amount of *already boiling* salted water. Again, simmer for 20 minutes. Test them for doneness by piercing with a fork. When the fork goes in easily, they are done.

VARIATION: POTATO SALAD Leftover boiled potatoes, both regular and new, can be cut into bite-sized chunks, mixed with finely chopped celery, minced shallot, and an optional finely chopped hard-boiled egg. (Peeling boiled new potatoes is optional, but they must at least be sliced.) Dress this mixture with mayonnaise (optimally homemade, page 149) into which a bit of Dijon mustard and salt and pepper have been added to taste. Cooked peas or peas and carrots make an interesting addition. By adding chopped fresh parsley or dill at serving time (rather than in the initial preparation), you help the salad taste fresh and look good longer.

*Making corn bread from scratch is not difficult—but if I wrote
that I often do so, I would be lying. The boxed mix is so
inexpensive (about 44 cents), so dependable, and so
incredibly easy to make—and really does taste so good, particularly
in the variations described below—that this is one convenience
food worth keeping on hand. Each little box of corn muffin mix
(Jiffy and Martha White are the two leading brands: Jiffy is sweeter;
Martha White is more traditionally "Southern") makes an 8 × 8-inch
pan of corn bread in the toaster oven.*

SERVES 4

NONSTICK COOKING SPRAY
ONE $8^1/2$-OUNCE BOX CORN MUFFIN MIX
1 LARGE EGG, AT ROOM TEMPERATURE
$^1/_3$ CUP MILK

PREHEAT YOUR TOASTER OVEN to 400 degrees F. Spray an 8 × 8-inch baking dish with nonstick cooking spray.

Prepare the mix according to package directions, substituting yogurt for the milk (if you like it tangy), adding an extra tablespoon of
sugar or honey (if you like more sweetness), and/or a tablespoon of
cornmeal (if you want more crunch). If the top is browning un-
evenly, turn the pan around halfway through the baking time,
which is a little less than the 20 minutes suggested on the package.

VARIATION: BLUEBERRY CORN BREAD Add up to 1 cup blueberries to the batter, plus 2 tablespoons sugar and 1 teaspoon vanilla extract. For a scintillating effect, sprinkle cinnamon sugar generously on top before baking according to package directions.

VARIATION: CHILE-CHEESE CORN BREAD This very rich, much-loved "white trash" recipe makes excellent ballast for an otherwise light meal, like soup.

NONSTICK COOKING SPRAY

3 LARGE EGGS, AT ROOM TEMPERATURE

ONE 4-OUNCE CAN CHOPPED GREEN CHILES, DRAINED

1 CUP CORN, CANNED AND DRAINED OR COOKED AND DRAINED

ONE $8^1/2$-OUNCE BOX CORN MUFFIN MIX

12 TABLESPOONS ($1^1/2$ STICKS) UNSALTED BUTTER, MELTED

1 TEASPOON BAKING POWDER

1 TEASPOON SALT

1 CUP SOUR CREAM, LIGHT SOUR CREAM, OR WHOLE YOGURT

1 CUP GRATED MONTEREY JACK CHEESE (4 OUNCES)

PREHEAT YOUR TOASTER OVEN to 350 degrees F. Spray a 9 × 9-inch pan with nonstick cooking spray.

Beat the eggs; add the chiles, corn, and corn muffin mix. Add the remaining ingredients and mix again until blended. Pour the mixture into the prepared pan. Bake for 45 minutes, or until golden brown, turning the pan halfway through cooking if necessary so that the top browns evenly. Cool the corn bread on a rack for 5 minutes before cutting it into squares.

Rice cooks up well in a nonstick saucepan so long as you keep the heat low and don't disturb the rice while it is cooking. The proportions are two parts low-sodium broth (or water) to one part long-grain white or brown rice.

Bring the liquid to a boil, add the rice (and a small quantity of unsalted butter or oil if desired), cover, lower the heat, and simmer very gently for 20 minutes (for white rice) or 45 minutes (for brown rice). Turn off the heat and let the rice sit for another 5 minutes (for white rice) and 15 minutes (for brown rice) to dry out and become fluffy. Both white and brown rice can benefit from being sautéed briefly in oil or unsalted butter before boiling, so if you like your rice with a slightly toasty flavor, consider doing so.

Instant couscous is even easier than rice to prepare. The proportions are one part instant couscous to one part broth. Simply pour the couscous into the boiling broth, cover, let it sit for 5 minutes, and then fluff with a fork. As with rice, adding unsalted butter and/or oil is optional.

Fluffy Rice Tip: While your cooked rice is sitting, you can help make it even fluffier by placing a clean, dry kitchen towel between the rice pot and the lid. The towel absorbs the steam escaping from the rice. The rice becomes lighter, drier, and fluffier as a result.

Brown Rice Storing Tip: Refrigerate raw brown rice, since the oils in this grain may otherwise go rancid. Smell the rice before cooking to make sure that it's still fresh. If it has a stale odor, discard it.

Salad Greens

STORING AND KEEPING LETTUCE in a small kitchen is certainly a challenge. While hearts of romaine lettuce are (apart from that old standby, iceberg) perhaps the most compact and long-lived salad green currently available, watercress, endive, fennel, carrot, celery hearts, and English cucumber all store well and afford a better variety of flavors. A paper towel placed inside a locking plastic storage bag with cleaned greens helps to absorb excess moisture and prolong the life of the greens. Fresh herbs (except for delicate ones like basil) do well with similar treatment.

FASTEST ENDIVE SALAD

Top individual leaves of endive with Roquefort and chopped, toasted walnuts for an easy, finger-friendly cheese-and-salad course for a party. Use very finely chopped fresh parsley for garnish, if desired.

CRUNCHY FENNEL–PARMESAN SALAD

Wash a bulb of fennel, then trim and slice it fine (you will need a sharp knife). Toss the slices in a bowl with olive oil, salt, and freshly ground black pepper. Shave a generous amount of Parmesan cheese over it, using a vegetable peeler, right before serving. Finely chopped fennel fronds make a quick green garnish for this otherwise very pale salad. One bulb of fennel serves two.

WATERCRESS OR ARUGULA "STEALTH SALAD"

Putting washed and dried salad greens underneath your main course means everything in your meal goes happily (and stealthily) onto one plate. Watercress, which is peppery and crisp even when exposed to hot foods, goes well with simply roasted or sautéed meats or poultry. So does arugula. The juices from whatever you have roasted or sautéed become a simple dressing for the greens.

REAL GERMAN COLESLAW

This is a great recipe for people who enjoy angry chopping and mashing as a form of stress relief. If the idea of shredding a cabbage leaves you nonplussed (and yes, it's messy), just buy packaged, preshredded cabbage at your supermarket or vegetable stand. Because of the oil and vinegar dressing, this salad lasts very well in the refrigerator (in a sealed container, please: it's odorous). If you doubt you can consume so much coleslaw within 2 weeks, you can easily halve the recipe.

Note: It's best not to use olive oil in this recipe because its flavor is too strong.

SERVES 6

1 SMALL HEAD CABBAGE (ABOUT 2 POUNDS)

1 TABLESPOON SALT

4 MEDIUM SHALLOTS, FINELY CHOPPED

3 TABLESPOONS CIDER VINEGAR

1 TEASPOON SUGAR

3 TABLESPOONS SAFFLOWER OR PEANUT OIL

1 TABLESPOON CARAWAY SEEDS

CUT THE CABBAGE IN HALF, wash it, trim away the tired exterior leaves, and cut out the solid white core from each half. Finely shred the remaining cabbage. Place the shredded cabbage in a mixing bowl, add the salt, and pound the cabbage with a potato masher (or a sturdy mug) until it becomes a little less stiff. Let it sit for about 15 minutes, pour off any accumulated juices, then add the shallots.

Mix together the vinegar and sugar, pour this over the cabbage mixture, and toss well. Let the cabbage sit for another 15 minutes, then add the oil and caraway seeds and toss again.

Cabbage Chopping Tip: Chopping cabbage can be a slippery, dangerous, messy business. Keep your chopping board glued to the countertop by setting it atop a dampened kitchen towel. Always halve your cabbage before shredding it: it's easier to core the cabbage, and half a cabbage will sit securely on the chopping board while you shred it. Make sure your (chef's) knife is sharp. Finally, pause every few slices to collect the shredded cabbage and place it in your bowl—doing so will prevent cabbage shreds from flying all over your countertop and floor.

VARIATION: COLESLAW SALAD Real German Coleslaw can be served atop a softer, contrasting salad green. Together the two make a robust and hearty salad.

English cucumbers are longer and more expensive than regular cucumbers, and are shrink-wrapped in plastic rather than waxed— they have an easily digested skin, so they need not be peeled or seeded unless you care to do so. If you'd like to use regular cucumbers in this recipe, you'll need 2 cucumbers. Just peel and seed them before slicing them. This salad will last 2 weeks in the refrigerator. If you grow tired of the original dressing, drain the cucumbers and toss them with some sour cream, salt, pepper, and a little more fresh dill.

SERVES 4

1 ENGLISH CUCUMBER, WASHED

2 TABLESPOONS SALT

4 TABLESPOONS SUGAR

3/4 CUP CIDER VINEGAR

2 TABLESPOONS FINELY CHOPPED FRESH DILL

THINLY SLICE THE CUCUMBER. Dissolve the salt in enough cold water to cover the cucumber. Add the cucumber slices and let sit for 30 minutes. Drain and rinse the slices thoroughly to rid them of excess salt.

To make the dressing, dissolve the sugar in 3/4 cup cold water. Add the vinegar and dill and stir to mix. Pour it over the cucumbers. For best flavor, let the salad sit for 1 hour before serving.

BIG-BATCH COOKING

Since cooking in a really small kitchen is an ordeal, why not do it just once in a really big batch? That way you can enjoy the hard-won results over the course of many later, easily defrosted meals. (This strategy is a crucial part of sailboat cooking, since nobody likes chopping onions while close-hauled.) Here is a group of recipes designed so that you can eat some of the food on the day you cook it, but save the rest for later in your refrigerator or freezer. Keep in mind that each recipe can also be the basis of a very good dinner party. Recipes that are particularly well suited to dinner parties are indicated by a corkscrew symbol .

MOLE-STYLE CHILI

*Divided up into 1-pint containers and frozen,
this all-meat recipe becomes the basis of any number of
other fast dishes for toaster oven or microwave. Ancho chili powder
and cocoa give the chili a distinctively rich, dark, smoky flavor.
A combo pack of meat loaf mix consists of 1 pound
ground beef, $^1/_2$ pound ground veal, $^1/_2$ pound ground pork;
they are sold this way at most supermarkets.*

SERVES 12

2 LARGE ONIONS, CHOPPED

$^1/_4$ CUP OLIVE OIL

TWO 2-POUND MEAT LOAF COMBO PACKS

2 TEASPOONS KOSHER SALT

$^1/_3$ CUP ANCHO CHILI POWDER

3 TABLESPOONS GROUND CUMIN

3 TABLESPOONS DRIED OREGANO

2 TABLESPOONS GROUND CINNAMON

3 TABLESPOONS UNSWEETENED COCOA POWDER

$1\,^1/_2$ TEASPOONS CAYENNE PEPPER

8 GARLIC CLOVES, MINCED

ONE 32-OUNCE CAN TOMATO JUICE

3 CUPS LOW-SODIUM BEEF BROTH

2 TABLESPOONS YELLOW CORNMEAL

COOK THE ONIONS in the oil in a Dutch oven or heavy soup pot for 20 minutes. Simultaneously, break up the meat, place it in another large pan, sprinkle the salt over it, and cook it down, breaking apart the meat with a wooden spoon as it cooks.

At the end of the 20 minutes, sprinkle the onions with the seasonings and garlic and stir. Add the meat. Let this mixture cook an additional 5 minutes. Don't rush this part; you really want to let the spices cook in the onions and hot fat to develop their full flavor along with the beef. Time the 5 minutes if necessary and stir diligently, because the spices may stick to the bottom of the pan. (If they do, that's okay.)

Add the tomato juice and beef broth and bring the mixture to a boil, scraping up any bits stuck to the bottom of the pan and incorporating them into the sauce. Lower the heat and let simmer, uncovered, for 1 hour, placing a spatter screen over the pot to minimize any greasy mess.

Stir in the cornmeal, cook an additional 3 minutes, and cool. Taste to correct seasoning when warm. If freezing, divide into containers and freeze.

VARIATION: MOLE-STYLE CHILI WITH BLACK BEANS For every 2 cups of chili, add one 10-ounce can black beans, drained and rinsed. Reheat thoroughly, correct seasoning, and top with sour cream, grated cheese (Jack, Cheddar, or Gruyère), and finely chopped shallot or scallion and/or finely chopped fresh parsley or cilantro. Serve with One-Pot, No-Mess Corn Bread (page 162), warmed flour tortillas, or rice (page 164).

VARIATION: MOLE-STYLE CHILI STUFFED BAKED POTATO Serve the chili (with or without beans) on a Baked Potato (page 155), accompanied by grated Jack, Cheddar, or Gruyère cheese, running it under the broiler to brown the top if you like. Top with sour cream and/or finely chopped shallot or scallion, as well as finely chopped fresh parsley and/or cilantro.

VARIATION: MOLE-STYLE CHILI NACHOS Arrange restaurant-style corn chips in an ovenproof dish. Distribute a spoonful of chili (with or without black beans) on each chip, and top with a judicious amount of chopped jalapeños and grated Jack, Cheddar, or Gruyère cheese. Broil, microwave, or bake the nachos at 400 degrees F until the cheese melts and the entire dish is hot. Garnish with sour cream, finely chopped tomato, chopped fresh coriander, and/or finely chopped chives, and serve with salsa.

VARIATION: MOLE-STYLE CHILI BURRITO In a large flour tortilla, place some heated chili (with or without beans), cooked warm rice, and grated Jack, Cheddar, or Gruyère cheese, along with shredded lettuce and finely chopped tomato. Fold in the ends, roll up the tortilla into a large package, and eat it, either with your hands (tricky) or with a knife and fork. Salsa, guacamole, and/or sour cream are good accompaniments.

VARIATION: MOLE-STYLE CHILI "LASAGNA" WITH CORN TORTILLAS Preheat the oven to 375 degrees F. Rub a small amount of olive oil on a 9-inch pie plate, and a small amount of olive oil on 3 corn tortillas. Starting with a corn tortilla, stagger layers of tortilla, chili, shredded Jack cheese, finely chopped shallot, and Spanish-style tomato sauce (one 8-ounce can will be plenty), another tortilla, and so forth. When you reach the final tortilla, top it with just cheese and tomato sauce. Bake for about 25 minutes, or until the cheese is bubbling and the tortillas are crunchy and crusty. Remove from the oven and serve with hot sauce and sour cream.

BIG BATCH RAGÙ

Ragù, the queen of pasta sauces, is perfect for the small kitchen in many ways: It's made from simple ingredients, freezes beautifully, creates no vaporized grease or smoke because it requires no browning, and needs no high heat to cook, so it is easily made on a stove with small burners. You can serve ragù on many small-shaped pastas, including rigatoni, ziti, conchiglie, and rotelle.

MAKES ABOUT 10 CUPS

$1/2$ CUP FINELY CHOPPED SHALLOT OR ONION

$1/2$ CUP FINELY CHOPPED CELERY

$1/2$ CUP FINELY CHOPPED CARROT

12 TABLESPOONS ($1 1/2$ STICKS) UNSALTED BUTTER

$3/4$ CUP OLIVE OIL

3 POUNDS GROUND CHUCK

SALT

4 CUPS DRY WHITE WINE

2 CUPS MILK

$1/2$ TEASPOON NUTMEG

8 CUPS CANNED ITALIAN CHOPPED TOMATOES WITH JUICE (TWO 28-OUNCE CANS PLUS HALF A 15-OUNCE CAN), PREFERABLY SAN MARZANO BRAND

2 BAY LEAVES

IN A DUTCH OVEN OR HEAVY SOUP POT, sauté the shallot, celery, and carrots in the butter and oil until the shallot is translucent. Add the beef and salt and mix, cooking the beef down gently. Do not brown it. When the beef is cooked, add the wine and turn the heat up to medium. When the wine has evaporated, add the milk and nutmeg. Stir the mixture and let it cook until the milk, too, has evaporated. Then add the tomatoes and bay leaf and stir again. Turn the heat to low and simmer very, very gently, uncovered, for 4 hours, using a spatter screen to minimize the mess (which will be minimal). When done, taste and correct salt.

Low Heat Cooking Tip: If your stove won't give you a low enough flame to cook your ragù (or soup or stew) at the barest simmer, you can lift your pot and diffuse the flame by making a ring of aluminum foil and setting it atop the burner. Use about 3 feet of foil scrunched into a rope $3/4$ inch thick. Form a ring the size of the burner, set the ring atop the burner, and set the pot atop the ring. You can also buy an inexpensive diffuser.

VARIATION: RAGÙ SLOPPY JOE While ragù is best over pasta, it can be reheated and eaten as a sandwich on a toasted crusty roll or piece of hollowed-out French bread. If you like, top with shredded mozzarella or Jack cheese and broil in the toaster oven.

VARIATION: BOWL OF RAGÙ Think of it as chili, Italian-style. Grate some Parmesan cheese over the top and dig in. Accompany it, of course, with a hunk of good Italian bread.

VARIATION: RAGÙ BAKED POTATO The Irish answer to pasta Bolognese. Start with a Baked Potato (page 155), add heated ragù, and accompany with either wine or beer.

CHOUCROUTE GARNI

Choucroute garni is a very good dinner party meal—enough like the weenies-and-sauerkraut of our collective childhood that just about everyone will eat it. You prepare the choucroute (braised sauerkraut) the night before and then just reheat it with the sausages and meats on the evening of the party. If you aren't in the mood for a party, just prepare the choucroute, which keeps beautifully, eating a little bit now by yourself (your lonely little bratwurst will be transformed into a full and robust meal), and saving the rest for the moment your mood improves. If you are feeling expansive, the recipe can be doubled; it will fit in the same Dutch oven.

Serve the choucroute directly from the Dutch oven at the table, accompanied by boiled potatoes, Dijon mustard, and a chilled dry Alsatian or German Riesling. A simple watercress salad dressed only with olive oil and a little salt makes a very refreshing follow-up. The best possible sauerkraut is important here; if you can't buy it directly from the barrel, you can find decent refrigerated sauerkraut in most supermarkets.

SERVES 4

ONE 1 QUART CONTAINER (OR ONE 2-POUND BAG) FRESH SAUERKRAUT

4 OUNCES SLAB BACON, RIND REMOVED, CUT INTO MATCHSTICK-SIZED PIECES

2 TABLESPOONS UNSALTED BUTTER, LARD, OR DUCK FAT

3 LARGE SHALLOTS, THINLY SLICED

1 CARROT, SCRAPED AND THINLY SLICED

FRESHLY GROUND BLACK PEPPER

3 STEMS FRESH PARSLEY

1 BAY LEAF

3 JUNIPER BERRIES (OPTIONAL)

1 SHOT OF GIN

$^1/_2$ CUP DRY RIESLING (OR, IF YOU'D RATHER NOT OPEN A BOTTLE OF WINE, $^1/_3$ CUP DRY VERMOUTH)

2 TO 3 CUPS LOW-SODIUM CHICKEN BROTH

SALT

1 TABLESPOON CARAWAY SEEDS

8 GERMAN SAUSAGES (BRATWURST, KNACKWURST, BAUERNWURST, WIENERS, OR POLISH KIELBASA LINKS)

4 CURED, SMOKED, AND COOKED PORK CHOPS (KASSELER RIPPCHEN), ABOUT 8 OUNCES EACH, OR 2 HAM STEAKS, ABOUT 7 OUNCES EACH, RINDS TRIMMED AND CUT IN HALF.

PREHEAT YOUR OVEN (if you have one) to 350 degrees F.

Drain the sauerkraut in a sieve and rinse it in several changes of cold water, letting it soak for several minutes between rinsings. The idea is to get rid of the briny, smelly liquid in which the sauerkraut has been preserved, leaving only a neutral, odorless preserved cabbage behind.

In a Dutch oven, cook down the bacon pieces in the fat. Add the shallots and carrot. Cook over low heat for about 10 minutes; do not let the shallots brown. Stir in the sauerkraut. Grind some pepper into it; add the fresh parsley, bay leaf, juniper berries if using, gin, Riesling, and chicken broth. Simmer, add salt to taste and the caraway seeds, cover, and cook in the oven (if you have one) or over a very, very low flame (if you don't) for $3^1/2$ hours, checking occasionally to see that it does not dry out on the bottom (poke down to the bottom with a spoon to check). If the mixture is too dry, add more chicken broth, Riesling, or water.

(If you have trouble keeping the flame low enough to cook the choucroute atop the stove, check out the Low Heat Cooking Tip on page 177.)

Place the meats on top of the choucroute for the last 30 minutes of cooking. (For extra credit, sauté the sausages in a little oil before placing them atop the choucroute to give them added color and presence.)

Spice Bag Tip: To keep yourself from losing the parsley, juniper berries, and bay leaf in your choucroute, place them into a paper coffee filter, tie it off with a thread, and bury the bag in the sauerkraut—then just remove the bag before serving.

DESSERTS

Meals are best when they end sweetly, even with something as simple as cookies or fruit. When you're dining alone, desserts provide a sense of closure to an evening's eating, and keep you from heading back to the fridge for that late-night snack. As for dining with company—well, you can't have people over without finishing the meal with a flourish. Look for a for especially festive party desserts.

MARZIPAN BAKED APPLE

Baked apples are delicious whether served hot, warm, or at room temperature—with cream, ice cream, whipped cream, custard . . . or just by themselves. Make a few of them at a time to keep on hand for quick, homey snacks. Since they taste great at room temperature, they are perfect for a make-ahead dinner party.
Marzipan is a sweetened almond paste available in the baking section of most supermarkets; the best-known brand in the U.S. is Odense, which comes in a 7-ounce tube.

SERVES 2

2 APPLES (GOLDEN DELICIOUS RECOMMENDED; IT HOLDS ITS SHAPE BEST)

6 TABLESPOONS MARZIPAN

2 TABLESPOONS UNSALTED BUTTER

2 CINNAMON STICKS

4 GREEN CARDAMOM PODS, CRACKED (OPTIONAL)

1 TABLESPOON SUGAR

to 350 degrees F.

Core each apple, then cut a line or strip through the skin, either with a knife or vegetable peeler, about a third of the way down the apple (this is to keep the apple from bursting while it cooks). Fill the core of each apple with 3 tablespoons marzipan. Put 1 tablespoon butter on top of each apple and place the apples on an ovenproof dish. Arrange the cinnamon sticks and green cardamom pods if using in the dish with the apples. Dissolve the sugar in $1/4$ cup warm water and pour it over the apples. Cover the dish with tinfoil and bake for 1 hour.

Remove the cooked apples with a spatula, being careful that the marzipan core does not slip out the bottom. Reduce the remaining sauce in a nonstick pan if you like. Pour the sauce, reduced or not, over the apples before serving.

The perfect batch of brownies for a neatnik. You line the pan with nonstick aluminum foil; when the brownies have cooled, just lift the foil and brownies out, leaving a clean dish behind. Then gently slice the brownies on the foil (thereby keeping your cutting board clean) and use the same foil to wrap up the sliced brownies. How neat is that?

MAKES SIXTEEN 2 × 2-INCH BROWNIES

1 STICK UNSALTED BUTTER

2 OUNCES (2 SQUARES) BAKING CHOCOLATE

1 CUP SUGAR

2 LARGE EGGS, BEATEN

$1/2$ CUP UNBLEACHED ALL-PURPOSE FLOUR

PINCH OF SALT

$1/2$ TEASPOON VANILLA EXTRACT OR DARK RUM

PREHEAT YOUR OVEN OR TOASTER OVEN to 350 degrees F.

Mold a piece of nonstick aluminum foil around the outside of an 8 × 8-inch pan, then flip the pan over and insert the foil. (If you don't have nonstick foil, spray your foil lightly with nonstick cooking spray.)

Melt the butter and chocolate in a nonstick saucepan over very low heat; alternatively melt them in a quart-sized measuring cup in the microwave (about 2 minutes on low). Add the sugar and then the eggs. Then incorporate the flour, salt, and vanilla.

Pour the batter into the foil-lined pan. Bake for 20 to 25 minutes, until just solid (keeping in mind that overbaked brownies will be dry and boring). Remove to a cooling rack. After the brownies have cooled, grasp the foil on each end of the dish and lift the foil and brownies out of the pan.

Place the foil on a cutting board and gently cut into 2-inch squares, but don't cut so deeply that you cut through the foil. Wrap leftover brownies in a second sheet of foil to freeze (these freeze well), or else serve at room temperature within a day.

VARIATION: EXTREME TOASTER-OVEN BROWNIES Add an extra 1 tablespoon flour to the batter. Break a $3^1/2$-ounce dark chocolate bar (preferably a Lindt Excellence 85% Cocoa Extra Fine Dark Chocolate bar) into small bits and stir into the batter before pouring it into the 8 × 8-inch dish. After they bake and have cooled, let these brownies chill in the fridge before slicing, since they are very fudgy.

Frozen Pie Trick

If you need a dessert but don't have time to make one, you can improve the appearance of a store-bought frozen pie by removing it from its foil pie pan and placing it into a glass or ceramic pie pan of the same size. With rare exceptions (namely deep-dish pies), commercially made fruit pies are 9 inches in diameter and fit perfectly into a 9-inch glass pie plate. Here is how to do it:

Remove the frozen pie from the carton and protective wrap.

Gently pull down on the pie pan edge to separate the pie shell crimp from the pie pan.

Place your left hand on the top of the pie and with your right hand gently flip the pie over. The frozen pie should release from the pan. If not, gently work the pan against the frozen pie until it releases free from the pan.

Place the frozen pie in the pie plate and bake as directed.

ITTY BITTY CAKE

Yes, it's silly to include a homemade cake recipe in a book about easy cooking—let's admit that right now. But there are moments in life when a homemade cake is both fun to make and a good way of expressing affection through loving hands at home. And this one is soooo simple.

The Itty Bitty Cake is a small, nearly foolproof cake that you can make in your toaster oven in an 8 × 8-inch baking dish. The batter can be beaten simply by hand, or else in a blender—but if you use a blender, just be aware that overmixing the batter will make the cake tough, so don't answer the telephone while it's running. (If possible, run the machine in short bursts.)

Following this recipe are two kinds of easy frosting that you put on the cake while it is still in the dish (and if baking a cake is simply too much cooking, by all means feel free to try these frostings on store-bought pound cake, which stores beautifully in the freezer and makes a great fast dessert). For fastest cleanup, see the Blender Cleanup Tip on page 83.

SERVES 4

NONSTICK COOKING SPRAY

1 CUP UNBLEACHED ALL-PURPOSE FLOUR

1 TEASPOON BAKING POWDER

$^1/_4$ TEASPOON SALT

$^1/_2$ CUP MILK

(continued)

1 TABLESPOON UNSALTED BUTTER

2 LARGE EGGS, AT ROOM TEMPERATURE

1 TEASPOON VANILLA EXTRACT

1 CUP SUGAR

PREHEAT YOUR TOASTER OVEN to 350 degrees F.

Spray your 8 × 8-inch baking dish with nonstick cooking spray, or if you plan on unmolding the cake and *really* don't want to take any chances, line the bottom of the pan with a piece of nonstick foil.

Put the flour, baking powder, and salt in a bowl and mix them together (if you want to sift them through a sifter to make sure there are no lumps in your flour and at the same time add a little extra volume, go ahead).

Heat the milk and butter together until the butter is melted (in your microwave or a saucepan). With your blender on low, running the machine in bursts, or else just in a bowl, beat the eggs with the vanilla until they are slightly thickened. Slowly add the sugar while continuing to beat. Add the flour mixture slowly until incorporated, then add the milk and butter mixture and mix well. This is going to be a thin batter.

Pour the batter into the prepared pan and bake for 25 minutes, until a toothpick inserted into the center of the cake comes out clean. Remove the cake from the oven and let it cool in the pan on a rack. Frost with one of the following toppings.

VARIATION: Another great thing to do with Itty Bitty Cake is: remove it from the pan, slice it in half with a serrated knife, spread the center with jam, put it back together on a cake plate, spread more jam on top, and garnish the glistening creation with fresh berries and whipped cream. This berry cake, however itty bitty, will nonetheless make a great *big* impression on your loved one.

Broiled Brown Sugar Topping

TOPS ONE 8 × 8-INCH CAKE STILL IN ITS PAN

3 tablespoons unsalted butter
3 tablespoons dark brown sugar
2 tablespoons cream
$1/2$ cup sweetened coconut, chopped walnuts, or a combination of both

In a small saucepan over low heat mix together the butter, dark brown sugar, cream, and coconut and/or walnuts. Spread the mixture over the warm cake and place it under the (toaster oven) broiler until bubbling and brown—but watch carefully to make sure it does not burn! Let the topping cool before eating, because molten sugar is really quite *dangerously* hot.

Ganache Frosting

Chilled ganache, which is really just your favorite melted bittersweet
chocolate bar (and once again mine is the Lindt Excellence
85% Cocoa Extra Fine Dark Chocolate bar), is a very versatile substance. If
you're not using ganache to frost an Itty Bitty Cake, you can drop it by
spoonfuls into cocoa powder to make a fast approximation of truffles (just
refrigerate them immediately to keep them in shape). You can also spread it on
a piece of baguette, or a croissant, or a graham cracker. Or else dilute it
to taste in hot milk (or half-and-half, adding more sugar as desired)
to make Weekend-in-Paris Hot Chocolate. This recipe makes
more than enough to fill and frost one Itty Bitty Cake.

MAKES 1 $^{1}/_{4}$ CUPS
$^{2}/_{3}$ cup heavy cream
two 3 $^{1}/_{2}$-ounce dark chocolate bars, broken into bits
1 tablespoon dark rum, bourbon, Cointreau, Kirsch, or espresso (optional)

BRING THE HEAVY CREAM TO A BOIL. Put the chocolate bits into a 2-cup storage
container, trying not to eat too much of it as you do so. When the cream is
boiling, pour it over the chocolate, then cover the container and let it stand for
10 minutes (really—time it).

When the 10 minutes are up, stir until the cream and chocolate combine into a smooth liquid, adding any additional flavoring you like. The mixture will seem very thin. Put it in the refrigerator until it is thick enough to spread over the cake—that is, when it has the consistency of the frosting on a doughnut. If the ganache becomes too thick to spread before you have a chance to frost the cake, let it sit at room temperature until it is spreadable again.

The easiest way to frost the cake is simply to spread the ganache on top. To create a maximum-ganache cake, remove the cake from the pan, slice it in half with a serrated knife, return the bottom layer to the 8 × 8-inch pan, spread on a layer of ganache, put the top layer on, and spread the remaining ganache on top. Since the cake stays in the baking dish, frosting it will be easy—no drips. Refrigerate the cake after frosting it to firm up the ganache.

If you don't like a heavily frosted cake, any leftover ganache will keep for at least a week refrigerated.

NOTE: The Lindt Excellence 85% Cocoa Extra Fine Dark Chocolate bar is sold at many supermarkets and drugstores for $1.99, available for a comparable price on the Web at www.lindtusa.com, and incidentally is worth every penny.

Here is another delicious small cake that is perfect for the toaster oven. It keeps beautifully, too. I found this super-moist and extra-spicy recipe (which calls for black pepper and dry mustard as well as ginger and molasses) in a church cookbook (Tremont Larger Parish Second Recipe Collections) *during a rain-soaked sailing trip to Mt. Desert Island, Maine.*

Don't try to cook this gingerbread in an 8 × 8-inch glass dish; you really do need a 9-inch square metal cake pan. Also, make sure that your butter is at room temperature, particularly if you intend to beat the mixture by hand.

MAKES ONE 9 × 9-INCH CAKE

NONSTICK COOKING SPRAY

$2^1/_2$ CUPS UNBLEACHED ALL-PURPOSE FLOUR

2 TEASPOONS BAKING SODA

$^1/_2$ TEASPOON SALT

1 TEASPOON GROUND CINNAMON

$1^1/_2$ TEASPOONS GROUND GINGER

$^1/_4$ TEASPOON GROUND CLOVES

$^1/_2$ TEASPOON DRY MUSTARD

$^1/_2$ TEASPOON FRESHLY GROUND BLACK PEPPER

8 TABLESPOONS (1 STICK) UNSALTED BUTTER, AT ROOM TEMPERATURE

$^1/_2$ CUP PACKED DARK BROWN SUGAR

2 LARGE EGGS, AT ROOM TEMPERATURE

1 CUP MOLASSES

1 CUP BOILING WATER

PREHEAT YOUR (TOASTER) OVEN to 375 degrees F. Spray a 9-inch square metal cake pan with nonstick cooking spray.

Combine the flour, baking soda, salt, cinnamon, ginger, cloves, mustard, and pepper in a large bowl; stir them together until blended and set aside. (If you like sifting, sift.)

In another bowl, cream together the butter and sugar until the mixture is light and fluffy. Add the eggs and beat well. Next beat in the molasses. Add the boiling water and beat again. Now combine the wet and dry ingredients and mix them together until you have a smooth batter. Pour the batter into the prepared pan.

Bake the gingerbread for 35 to 45 minutes, testing for doneness after 35 minutes by inserting a toothpick into the center of the gingerbread. If the toothpick comes out clean (that is, with no batter sticking to it) the gingerbread is done.

Remove the pan from the oven and place it on a baking rack for 5 minutes to cool. Then you can either remove the gingerbread from the pan and serve it from a plate, or else leave it in the pan and slice out squares of gingerbread as needed.

This is an exceptionally easy, sensationally good bread pudding full of bright orange flavor—and it's a natural for the toaster oven. Adjust the orange flavor through your choice of marmalade. I find a Seville orange marmalade is best for this recipe, but a stronger marmalade, such as a Dundee marmalade, might appeal to those who like a darker, more bitter orange flavor. American-made marmalades, blander and more sugary, will yield a much less trenchant (but adequately orange!) result.

SERVES 4

4 TABLESPOONS ($^1/_2$ STICK) UNSALTED BUTTER, AT ROOM TEMPERATURE

SIX $^1/_2$-INCH-THICK SLICES STURDY WHITE BREAD (PEPPERIDGE FARM TOASTING WHITE OR ITS EQUIVALENT)

3 TABLESPOONS GOOD-QUALITY ORANGE MARMALADE (SEVILLE ORANGE MARMALADE IS BEST)

1 $^1/_2$ CUPS HALF-AND-HALF (OR 1 CUP HALF-AND-HALF AND $^1/_2$ CUP HEAVY CREAM)

3 LARGE EGGS, AT ROOM TEMPERATURE

GRATED ZEST OF 1 LARGE ORANGE

$^1/_2$ CUP SUGAR

1 TABLESPOON DEMERARA SUGAR, TURBINADO SUGAR ("SUGAR IN THE RAW"), OR WHITE SUGAR

2 TABLESPOONS FINELY CHOPPED CANDIED ORANGE PEEL (OPTIONAL)

PREHEAT YOUR OVEN to 350 degrees F. Spray an 8 × 8-inch baking dish with nonstick cooking spray.

Butter all 6 slices of the bread and spread the marmalade on 3 buttered slices; top them with the other 3 buttered slices so the butter faces the marmalade. Then butter the tops of the marmalade sandwiches. Slice the sandwiches into quarters (either squares or triangles, depending upon your artistic vision for the finished dish).

Arrange the sandwiches, butter side up, overlapping one another in the prepared baking dish. If they stand up a little, that's good: you want to make a toasty, crusty pudding.

Whisk the half-and-half, eggs, grated orange zest, and sugar together, and pour the mixture over the bread. Scatter the surface of the bread with the demerara sugar and candied peel if using.

Bake the pudding for 30 to 35 minutes. It should be puffy, golden, and crunchy on the top; if it isn't, or if you'd like a more toasty pudding, switch your (toaster) oven briefly to broil at the end of the cooking time. Remove the pudding and let it cool briefly on a rack. Serve the pudding while it is still puffy and warm, accompanied by heavy cream.

7

STRANGERS IN THE ITTY BITTY KITCHEN

We now COME TO THE GREATEST SMALL-KITCHEN CHALLENGE OF THEM ALL: DINNER GUESTS. FOR, AS EVERY SMALL-KITCHEN COOK KNOWS, THERE'S NOTHING TOO DIFFICULT ABOUT COOKING AND SERVING A MEAL TO PLEASE *YOURSELF*. IT'S ONLY WHEN OTHER PEOPLE ENTER YOUR HOME THAT LIFE IN THE KITCHEN SPINS TRULY AND COMPLETELY OUT OF CONTROL.

BUT, IN FACT, HAVING PEOPLE OVER FOR DINNER IS RELATIVELY SIMPLE IF YOU ADMIT FROM THE OUTSET THAT WHAT YOU ARE ATTEMPT-ING—NAMELY, TO ENTERTAIN ON A GRAND SCALE WITH EFFORTLESS GRACE IN AN APARTMENT BETTER SUITED TO HOBBITS THAN TO HU-MANS—IS REALLY JUST BASICALLY IMPOSSIBLE. ONCE YOU'VE ACCEPTED THAT YOU'RE TRYING TO DO SOMETHING WELL BEYOND THE REALM OF all possibility, you are free to start developing those many little tricks, strategies, and outright deceptions that will provoke wonder and amazement in all of your guests.

The Good News about Itty Bitty Entertaining

CHALLENGED AS YOU MAY BE BY YOUR SMALL SPACE, you might keep in mind that your small digs give you a certain advantage. Done right, a close-quarters dinner party can intensify feelings of togetherness, coziness, and intimacy between friends. It can also foster introductions and promote openness among people in a way that larger and more intimidating get-togethers never really do. And, finally, if you throw your dinner party right, your home will impress others as uniquely desirable. For, believe it or not, many people with larger and more complicated lives find simple small-space living enormously attractive: Louis XV, for example, much preferred cooking his own little dinner in a chafing dish in Madame de Pompadour's room to presiding over enormous state dinners at his own home, Versailles.

So (believe it or not) you have a great opportunity here to give delight through the very thing you yourself may consider your greatest liability: that snug little den you call home.

But doing so is going to require a whole lot of careful (and sometimes really sneaky) preparation.

Ahoy Mateys

NOBODY DOES SMALL-SPACE ENTERTAINING BETTER THAN A SAILOR. Entertaining at sea is nearly always fail-safe because (1) extremely cold, wet people are unusually content to huddle together in extremely small spaces, (2) exceptionally hungry and exhausted people will eat just about *anything* with relish, (3) sailors really *do* love to drink *large* amounts of *any kind* of alcohol, and (4) sober or otherwise (and well fed or not), nearly everyone lucky enough to find him- or herself still afloat at the end of a long day on the water finds the damp, cramped, and basically uncomfortable experience of dining in a crawl space a great big thrilling adventure—one that merits toasting and celebrating well into the night.

The urban small-space host or hostess is considerably more challenged by entertaining in a tiny apartment, since no trip to a humble abode, however charming, can promise the thrills (and stimulating misery) of a day out on the high seas. Still, the following ideas on dinner preparation, all taken from life aboard a sailboat, may well come in handy the next time you ask your friends to dinner.

1. Make sure everything in your home is tidy, well-aired, and "shipshape." Doing so has a direct relation to the comfort of your guests, since many people can have panicky responses to messy or disorderly small spaces.
2. Be prepared. The less fussing you do, the more relaxed the evening will seem to others. Prior planning of every stage of

your meal is particularly important if you are hosting the dinner by yourself, since you'll need to play both captain and crew from the moment your guests arrive—taking coats, making conversation, attending to music, pouring drinks, and all that other fun stuff. So take preemptive action by having your table all set and your bar and your ice and your glasses and nibbles all ready.

3. Of course, it goes without saying that all your cooking will be completed well before the first guest arrives. Cooked foods for the main course can be placed in covered dishes on a warming tray close to your table. If you plan on serving a first course, set it out on the table before your guests arrive. Keep your dessert set up and ready in some discreet corner, too.

4. At the same time, be sure you've created a cozy and welcoming atmosphere. Make sure your place is comfortably lit, for example—not too bright, not too dark. If you live in monastic simplicity, consider enlivening your space with some kind of temporary decoration (a simple bunch of flowers will do wonders). Don't overdo it with candles, though, which can make a small room stuffy—and definitely avoid *scented* candles, which can be overwhelmingly stinky in small spaces.

5. Remain calm. Remember, people are much more alarmed by sudden movement and loud noise in smaller spaces. If you bustle and clank around too much in the kitchen, you are going to make people jumpy. Your music should be a little more soothing than usual for the same reason, particularly during mealtime. By creating an atmosphere of structure and deco-

rum, you'll soothe and reassure your guests, and they will relax that much more quickly into a warm and memorable evening.

6. Pick your passengers with care. Big personalities seem even bigger in small surroundings, so you really do need to make sure that everyone you have invited into your little home is compatible, both with each other and with the space, before you set out on your dinner party. This point is perhaps a little less crucial when applied to a three-hour meal than to a three-week cruise across the Pacific, but it is still an important consideration for anyone hoping to entertain gracefully and enjoyably in a very small space.

7. Above all, make having fun your top priority. Find something amusing to get the party going, and be ready for a good time when the doorbell rings—for just as a ship's passengers take their cues from the captain, so too will your guests take their cues from the host. Have a good time, and everyone else will fall in line and have a good time too.

A Brief Note on Dinner Party Food and Drink

CHOOSING WHAT TO MAKE FOR DINNER is part of the fun of holding a dinner party—but choosing the wrong thing can make entertaining tremendously difficult, so definitely choose with care. If you don't have any idea what to serve your friends, consult some of the recipes in this book: Those particularly good for small-space do-ahead dinners are indicated by a corkscrew symbol.

If you plan on serving drinks before dinner, some sort of nibbles are going to be necessary too, but they should be simple and stress-free—not things that need to be rushed out of a hot oven or passed around with napkins. Cheese crisps, roasted cashews, and some very good pitted olives, for example, can provide three very agreeable textures and flavors to guests, and at the same time eliminate all pesky toothpicks and stray olive pits from the scene.

Small kitchens and small homes really do require that you reconsider your choice of main course foods, too. By serving rich, hot, or heavy meals, you can quickly make your company feel trapped and overheated—particularly if you are entertaining at a warm time of year, can't easily regulate the heat, and/or can't open windows without creating a serious draft. So, in general, choose lighter foods, alternate hot and cold courses, and scale down your food plans to suit your smaller surroundings.

Also, whatever amount of food and drink you decide to serve, try to avoid those dishes that create extremely strong or pungent smells: boiled cabbage, fried garlic, and broiled oily fish, delicious though they may be, are not good choices in a small or stuffy space. Remember, too, that even if your cooking is completed well in advance, cooking odors can linger in your home. *You* may not notice them, but newly arrived guests almost certainly will! So, if possible, turn your oven off and shut down the kitchen a few minutes before the evening begins, and air out your apartment as thoroughly as you can before guests start to arrive. That way your home will be fresh and welcoming—and you, meanwhile, will be confident in greeting your guests.

Ambitious Cooking—Reconsidered

WHEN THE DESIRE TO SHOW OFF IS STRONG, remember, please, that culinary *modesty* can be equally impressive, and that in many instances discretion is the better part of valor. More effective, too, since most guests would rather have a relaxed and happy host than one who frets endlessly in the kitchen, however good his gravy may turn out. If cooking doesn't come easy for you, or if you become tense about last-minute timing, or if you (like most *normal* human beings) have a hard time cooking and talking at once, just simplify your meal plan—and, if possible, come up with a menu that will hold a good long time so you can visit with your guests before dinner begins.

Remember, too, that you are perfectly entitled to cut corners. People who preside over a tiny cook space are *definitely* allowed to avoid anything that could scorch, splatter, burn, explode, leak, drip, or burst into flame. They are also free to avoid anything that generates an undue amount of nasty, messy trash. Lobsters, artichokes, oysters, and Cornish game hens, lovely though they may be, are not for the IBK dinner party. Deep-frying, flame-broiling, and extensive engagement with a carving knife are similarly all best left to another time and place.

In general, the more simple, compact, and invisible your cooking is, the happier you, your apartment, and your guests are going to be.

If the inclination to cook *impressively* and *on a grand scale* persists (and in some people it amounts almost to a compulsion), consider that some people are actually *put off* by displays of culinary virtuosity—and that, alternatively, most friends really are perfectly content to be fed anything at all. Since your guests are probably more interested in talking to you than experiencing a culinary tour de force from a grumpy person who spends most of the evening alone in a tiny kitchen, why not humor them—and make your life a little easier into the bargain?

A Final Send-off from the British Royal Navy

PEOPLE WHO AREN'T USED TO SMALL ENVIRONMENTS, no matter how glad they are to be invited or how much they like the idea of small-space living, may find themselves unexpectedly tense because of the size of the quarters in which they suddenly find themselves thrust. The five-hundred-year-old British naval remedy for such tension belowdecks is, of course, that daily shipboard tot of grog (and, when all else fails, a flogging). The rum remedy works well in small apartments, too. So whenever you entertain in your itty bitty home, be sure to offer lots of good-quality drink at every stage of the evening. The result will be gratifying: with three cheers for the cook and a happy crew all around.

8

*M*any PEOPLE THINK THAT THE FIRST AND ONLY ACTIVITY THAT TAKES PLACE IN A KITCHEN IS COOKING. THIS MISUNDERSTANDING FOLLOWS LOGICALLY ENOUGH FROM THE PICTURE OF KITCHEN LIFE THAT COMES TO US THROUGH COMMERCIAL TELEVISION——WHERE MESSY BOWLS, CRUSTY PANS, AND GLOPPY UTENSILS ARE NEVER IN THE PICTURE FOR LONG, AND COUNTERTOPS ARE ALWAYS NEAT AND TIDY NO MATTER WHAT HAS JUST BEEN SLAUGHTERED, PLUCKED, AND COOKED.

IN REAL LIFE, HOWEVER, WE SPEND AS MUCH TIME ORGANIZING AND CLEANING OUR KITCHENS AS WE DO PREPARING FOOD IN THEM. AND IN AN ITTY BITTY KITCHEN YOU SEEM TO BE CLEANING UP CONSTANTLY, BOTH WHILE COOKING AND AFTER, NOT BECAUSE YOU *LIKE* IT, but because there's *simply no alternative.* Herewith, then, a chapter completely devoted to that unsung but necessary (and, to some, highly satisfying) activity called cleanup time.

The Dirty Truth about SBK Cleanup Time

EVEN IF YOU ENJOY CLEANING AND TIDYING, cleanup time in small kitchens can be much more difficult and frustrating, just because every aspect of that cleaning is complicated by the awkwardness and compression of the space. Moreover, small cooking spaces become much dirtier than large kitchens—not only because of the concentration of mess, but also because of the inevitable crowding of objects, which makes cleaning in, around, and underneath them so much more difficult. So your little kitchen is going to need not only a much more intense and concentrated cleaning effort from you but also a lot more patience. At the same time, persevere! Because kitchen cleanliness is much more vital to the small home than the large one, for the simple reason that *in a really small home there is simply no way to hide a mess.*

Many of us have grown up with no formal introduction to the surprisingly complicated world of housework.

As a result, we enter adulthood blissfully unaware of the proper way to wash a dish, organize a cupboard, or keep the refrigerator free of Listeria, shigella, or salmonella. So here's a primer. For a more thorough and serious look at housekeeping than this itty bitty book could ever manage, consult Cheryl Mendelson's authoritative (and very entertaining) *Home Comforts: The Art and Science of Keeping House* (New York: Scribner, 1999).

Small-Kitchen Dishwashing

WASHING UP IS, OF COURSE, the main and really *unavoidable* cleaning activity in which every itty bitty cook must engage, since (a) his or her kitchen is too small to allow anyone else to share the magic, and (b) few itty bitty kitchens have room for a (nonhuman) dishwasher. Small kitchens rarely even have room for the large or divided sink that makes old-fashioned dishwashing easiest. In many instances, there isn't even space for a proper dish-drying rack.

So, here is what you do.

Step One: Prepare

Here are your most needed supplies:

1. A small plastic washtub
2. Assorted dishwashing sponges, rags, or wands
3. Dish soap
4. A clean, absorbent dish towel and a hook near the sink on

which to hang it (and preferably several towels on several hooks)

5. A rubberized sink-bottom rack

Also useful:

1. A small metal or plastic basket, preferably with suction cup attachment, for holding dish sponges and washrags (such as the Oxo Good Grips Suction Sink Basket, $5.99 at www.oxo.com).
2. A sleek dish soap dispenser that will help minimize the "visual clutter" of the sink area (such as the stainless-steel Forma Koni Sink Pump, $16.50 at www.shopfosters.com).
3. A suction cup holder for keeping dish wands upright, thus stopping dish soap from leaking out—and also preventing them from cluttering the sink (Good Grips Suction brush holder, $2.99 at www.oxo.com).
4. Disposable surgical gloves, if desired, to protect manicures and so forth, available at any pharmacy. (These also come in handy when polishing silver, chopping jalapeño peppers, giving your dog a flea bath, or disposing of really scary leftovers. They can also be blown up like balloons to make short-notice party favors.)
5. Optional, and only if space allows: a drop-down over-sink dish rack (Closetmaid, part #3921; most readily available at Lowes, www.lowes.com, for $5.91) or in-sink dish drainer (www.containerstore.com, item # 10011443, $14.99).

Step Two: Take Preemptive Action to Minimize Small-Kitchen Dishwashing Trauma

1. Start with a clean sink. Sinks become mucky when dishes, glasses, and silverware sit in them and water and food particles collect around them, leading to stubborn stains, gooky slime, and hardened-on food crust. A simple rubberized rack at the bottom of the sink (or a stylish bubble silicone sink mat with hole, $12 at www.shopfosters.com) keeps dishes and other objects from touching the sink bottom, thus allowing water to flush through regularly and carry off the gunk and muck. Dishes and sink thus stay cleaner with a rack (and fewer things smash when dropped into the sink by accident, and the sink itself is protected from damage), so this little item is a very good investment.

2. Don't let dishes collect. The presence of even one dirty dish in your all-too-visible sink gives the kitchen (and, by extension, your apartment) a messy look. So wash up after every meal or snack. If you choose to wait for a batch of dishes before washing, at least rinse the dishes free of food and then set them to soak in a basin of soapy hot water. This gives the (false but reassuring) illusion of "cleaning in progress."

3. Make a conscious effort to minimize dish usage. It doesn't take a rocket scientist to realize that the fewer dishes you use, the fewer you need to clean. A good small-kitchen cook cleans up as he goes and keeps dish usage minimal.

Step Three: Wash Them Dishes

1. After mealtime, scrape food waste into the garbage, and then stack your dishes on the countertop (or the appliance top) closest to the sink. Find another clear space somewhere in the kitchen on which you will be able to put your freshly washed dishes.

2. If you have a telephone headset and are naturally talkative, put on the headset and dial a friend, preferably one who won't mind the sounds of rushing water and a little random clinking. Or listen to the radio. Or else just zone out and meditate on where your life has been taking you lately.

3. Fill your washtub with hot soapy water. Keep the part of the sink not taken up by the tub open for rinsing dishes in hot, free-flowing tap water. Have extra dish soap and your sponge, washrag, and/or dish wand at the ready. If you want to protect that gorgeous manicure of yours, now is the time to don your disposable gloves!

4. Wash items in order: glasses first to avoid breakage, then plates, then mugs, then utensils, then silverware. End with the big stuff: pots, baking dishes, and cutting boards. Scrub your dishes in the hot soapy water, and then rinse them under hot tap water. Wash as many things as you can until you run out of space on which to set the washed things. Then pause in your washing labors, turn off the tap, take a moment for yourself (stretching if necessary), and pick up a clean, dry dish towel.

5. Dry each washed item thoroughly and put it away in its designated place. Remember that while putting dishes away wet can help bacteria to breed and putting glasses away wet may cause them to spot, slightly damp dishes and glasses will do their final drying well enough in a cupboard, particularly if the shelving has been lined with ventilating pads for glassware and vertical stacking props for dishes.

6. Return to washing and rinsing until once again you run out of countertop space for clean dishes. Turn off the tap, stretch a little, pick up the dish towel, and again start drying and putting away.

7. Repeat until no more dishes remain.

8. When all done, empty the soapy washtub, wipe down the sink and the countertops, and replace the dish towel on its hook so that it can air-dry properly. Rinse and squeeze out sponges and dishrags and set them to dry as well.

9. Since the most dangerous kitchen pathogens lurk in sponges and washrags, they must be disinfected daily. If you have a microwave, place a dry sponge in the microwave and run it on high for 30 seconds; wet sponges require a full minute. Cotton washrags should be microwaved for 1 minute on high if dry, or for 3 minutes if wet. If you have no microwave, sanitize sponges and washrags using a solution of 1 tablespoon chlorine bleach per quart of hot water. Keep in mind also that it's recommended to discard your kitchen sponge every week, and to replace used dish towels with freshly washed dish towels at least once a week.

I tty bitty kitchens are not always without automatic appliances; in fact, even as apartment kitchens diminish in size, they are increasingly being stocked with every possible convenience, for the simple reason that an appliance is much easier to come by (and much less expensive) than extra real estate square footage. If you are blessed with a dishwasher in your tiny kitchen space (and the GE Spacemaker [www.geappliances.com] and more upscale Miele Slimline [www.miele.com] dishwashers both come in sizes as small as 18 inches, so it's really not impossible to imagine), here are four important tips for maximizing the usefulness of this miraculous dish-hiding, dish-cleansing machine:

1. Empty the dishwasher as soon as it has completed its run—for the simple reason that, if you have clean dishes in the dishwasher, you have no place to put dirty dishes and you will naturally stack them in the sink or leave them around the house. Follow this one very basic but life-changing rule, and your kitchen (and home) will always look great (or at least better).

2. Give yourself permission to run the machine with smaller loads of dishes. Yours is not in a large and busy household, and you haven't got that many dishes; if you were to wait until your dishwasher was fully loaded, you would probably use

up every dish in your home before running it, and in the meantime you'd have to remove and wash many things by hand since you would need them for your meal preparation.

3. Consider using a gentler dishwasher detergent, shorter dish cycles, and smaller amounts of dish soap per load. Smaller homes with limited air circulation are more strongly affected by dishwasher fumes, which often cause headaches and dizziness. Moreover, gentler detergents in smaller quantities save wear and tear on your dishes—and few of your dishes (if any) need that full-bore "potscrubber" treatment. (Using less soap and less electricity is gentler on the environment as well.)

4. Remember that your dishwasher can also be used to heat dishes before mealtimes, simply by running them through the "dry" cycle. It can also be used to sanitize chopping boards and deep clean any number of other washable home furnishings, such as storage bins, vases, buckets, and utility sponges.

Flatware Tip for Your Dishwasher: To save time sorting clean flatware, sort the dirty flatware as you put it into the dishwasher: teaspoons with teaspoons, forks with forks. Unloading the dishwasher goes much faster as a result.

Weekly or Biweekly Chores

NOW THAT WE HAVE TACKLED DISHWASHING, let's look at some of the other care-and-maintenance activities that every little kitchen will inevitably require.

1. *Clutter control and countertop reclamation*. Every few days take a look at your countertops and note what has accumulated upon them. It's probably not related to cooking. Spend the necessary time either finding a home for these things or else getting rid of them.

2. *Is there a place for everything? Is everything in its place?* The more cooking you do, the more you accumulate **STUFF**. If you are spending a lot of time trying to put things away, it's probably because you once again have too much. Reconsider the current contents of those cupboards—and edit, edit, edit.

3. *Pantry and fridge patrol*. Clean sticky residues off frequently used food containers such as sugar bowls, jam pots, honey jars, and water filtration pitchers. And while you're there, get preemptive with items on the edge of doom—don't wait for them to spoil. Instead, ask yourself if these items really stand a chance of being eaten between now and the moment they become toxic.

4. *Wipe down*. A certain urban grunge is going to accumulate in your kitchen countertops, walls, floors, appliances, and cupboards even if you clean up after every meal. Wiping down

these surfaces with a gentle, pleasantly scented countertop spray can keep your kitchen looking and feeling fresh and loved between uses.

5. *Sanitize.* If you work with raw meats, poultry, or eggs in your kitchen, you need to worry about illness-causing bacteria. All surfaces that come in contact with these raw foods should be washed down as soon and as thoroughly as possible with hot soapy water, then sanitized with a solution made up of 1 teaspoon chlorine bleach per quart of hot water. Use this bleach solution to sanitize your sink and garbage pail on a regular basis, too.

6. *Pest check.* Your own kitchen may be super-clean, but who knows what's swarming through the apartments next door? Moreover, most packaged grains, flours, and dried fruits (no matter how tightly you have sealed them) will eventually begin to hatch out bugs, grubs, beetles, and other pantry pests. So keep an eye out for critters and their spoor, and discard anything that appears to be infested.

7. *Odor control.* Different areas of your kitchen are going to generate smells no matter how careful you are. Even a meticulously policed refrigerator can develop an odor based on its contents, particularly if it is stocked with highly seasoned prepared foods, ripe cheese, and other spoilage-prone dairy products, or even such innocent-looking fruits as melon or papaya. Sealed spices will likewise leak strong odors into your cupboards as their volatile oils disperse over time; some are pungent enough to settle permanently into your cabinetry.

While odors often indicate that cleaning or purging is needed, odor-neutralizing baking soda boxes will also help keep basic food smells in check. They cost very little and work like a charm. So buy them frequently, change them every month or so, and pour older boxes down your drains to help keep them fresh-smelling, too.

8. *Clean sweep.* While you will probably only need to mop and wax your kitchen floor on a monthly basis, it wouldn't kill you to sweep, Swiffer, or dust-bust as needed—particularly if you have a kibble-crunching, water-dribbling, dirt-tracking, hair-shedding pet. If you're feeling really ambitious, consider giving that floor a quick wipe-down with a paper towel dampened with a little all-purpose cleaner. It takes just a second and it really makes a difference.

9. *Air and deodorize.* If you cook regularly in your home, cooking smells are inevitable and often very homey and pleasant—but they should not be encouraged to linger! Air your home regularly by opening the windows, particularly if your little kitchen lacks adequate ventilation: it's an important way of keeping the place clean, fresh, and healthy. Frequent laundering of the washable fabric in your home is important, too. Textiles that cannot be laundered can be refreshed with products such as Febreze spray, which uses a bona fide chemical reaction to neutralize odors. Frequent vacuuming with a hepafilter vacuum cleaner and the use of a trustworthy air filter are other good ways of keeping your small home clean, odorless, and lower in allergens.

While strong commercial solvents are useful in fighting grime, they can also have toxic effects—sometimes even inspiring dizziness, nausea, and skin rashes in the people who use them in very small spaces. The good news is, you don't always have to use them: A gentler cleaner can often keep your kitchen equally fresh and happy.

Alternative cleaning products are becoming justifiably popular (the best known commercial brands are Earth Friendly Products, www.ecos.com; Naturally Yours, www.naturallyyoursstore.com; Caldrea Home Care, www.caldrea.com; and Mrs. Meyer's Clean Day, www.mrsmeyers.com). But if you'd like to be thrifty as well as gentle, you can make your own homemade cleaning compounds as follows:

Cleaning refrigerator and freezer interiors: Use hot water with some regular dish soap. For additional freshness, add 4 tablespoons baking soda or 1 teaspoon chlorine bleach per quart of water.

Cleaning a regular oven: If your oven receives only light use, cleanings can be done with gentler cleaning formulas than those that are commercially available. Wet the interior surface and sprinkle on baking soda to form a paste. Rub gently with fine steel wool, then wipe off the scum with a damp cloth or sponge. Repeat if necessary. (Do not attempt this with self-cleaning or nonstick ovens.)

Cleaning and deodorizing a drain: **Pour 1 cup baking soda into your drain. Slowly drip warm water into the drain.**

Cleaning out a slow drain: **Pour 1 cup baking soda into your drain. Slowly pour 1 cup vinegar after it (it will fizz); cover the drain and let stand for 5 minutes, then follow with 1 gallon of boiling water.**

Cleaner for windows and mirrors: **Mix 4 parts water, 4 parts rubbing alcohol, and 1 part ammonia. Clean as you would with a commercial window cleaner.**

Strong all-purpose countertop cleaner: **Two cups of warm water with 1 tablespoon liquid laundry detergent and 1 tablespoon ammonia.**

Scouring powder for pots, stovetops, countertops, and inside refrigerators and freezers: **A simple paste of baking soda and water makes the gentlest possible scouring agent.**

Conclusion

Kitchen WORK IS, IN ITS BEST AND MOST RELAXING MOMENTS, A MEDITA-TIONAL PRACTICE—NOT JUST A SERIES OF MENIAL CHORES WE ENGAGE IN DAILY BY NECESSITY, BUT RATHER A WAY OF CONNECTING OURSELVES TO OUR HOME LIFE. FOR, BIG OR SMALL, A HOME CAN ONLY BECOME HOMELIKE THROUGH CONSTANT PRESENCE AND USE, AND THE HEART OF ALL ACTIVITY IN EVERY HOME (WHETHER ON LAND, ON WHEELS, OR AT SEA) IS THE KITCHEN. THE MOST SOULFUL KITCHENS IN THIS WORLD ARE IMPRESSIVE NOT BECAUSE OF THEIR LUX-URIES OR DIMENSIONS, BUT RATHER BECAUSE OF THE ENERGY, LOVE, AND ENTHUSIASM DEMONSTRATED ON A DAILY BASIS BY THEIR CARING AND CAREFUL INHABITANTS.

The organization and management of your very small kitchen is no easy thing, and mastering it will be an ongoing process. I hope this book helps you turn your ridiculously small cooking space into a truly functional kitchen. The ordering principles outlined in the first part of the book, done right, are done for good; but tinkering with your little kitchen is something that you will continue to do for as long as you own it. Finding new ways to simplify your storage, cooking, and cleaning setup will always be one of the most immediately satisfying forms of home improvement, because the effectiveness of that setup will be something you get to notice and enjoy with every passing mealtime.

Your shopping, cooking, entertaining, and cleanup skills will also continue to develop with experience—which is to say, by learning from your mistakes. (But rest assured there will be many happy triumphs, too—and many people who, whatever the results of your cooking, will be grateful to you for having shared them.) Reading about cooking and housekeeping is always a good way to learn how to cook and manage more efficiently—and doing so is particularly worthwhile if, like many of us, you grew up without much instruction in the domestic arts. Television programs about cooking are a valuable form of instructional entertainment, too. But there is really no substitute for actual hands-on cooking experience in that well-tuned little space of yours, the perfectly functional kitchen that functions against all odds. So go to it—proudly—and enjoy!

PROFESSIONAL ORGANIZING HELP:

National Association of Professional
  Organizers: www.napo.net

GENERAL RETAILERS:

Bed, Bath and Beyond:
  www.bedbathandbeyond.com
Home Depot: www.homedepot.com
K-Mart: www.kmart.com
Lowes: www.lowes.com
Macy's: www.macys.com
Sears: www.sears.com
Target Stores: www.target.com
Wal-Mart: www.walmart.com

SITES FOR HOME STORAGE AND ORGANIZATION
PRODUCTS:

Closetmaid products can be previewed
  through their official site,
  www.closetmaid.com, but must be
  purchased via retailers such as Lowes
  or The Container Store.
The Container Store:
  www.containerstore.com
Organize Everything: www.organize-
  everything.com
Ikea: www.ikea-usa.com
Organizes-it: www.organizes-it.com

KITCHEN EQUIPMENT SPECIALTY SITES:

3 M Command Removable Hooks:
  www.3m.com/us/home_leisure/command
Chef's Catalogue: www.chefscatalog.com
Compact Appliance:
  www.compactappliance.com
Cuisinart Products: www.cpokitchen.com
Fine Cookware: www.finecookware.com
Foster's Urban Homeware and Gourmet
  Cookware: www.Shopfosters.com

Frieling Kitchen Products:
  www.frieling.com
The Gadget Source:
  www.thegadgetsource.com
Oxo Kitchen Tools: www.oxo.com
Premium Knives: www.premiumknives.com
Smart Spin Storage System (compact plastic
  storage containers):
  www.asseenontvnetwork.com
U.S. Plastic (Industrial, commercial and con-
  sumer plastic products, including Rubber-
  maid products): www.usplastic.com
Zabar's Housewares: www.shopzabars.com

SITES FOR SPECIALTY FOOD PRODUCTS:

British groceries in America:
  www.ukgoods.com
Lindt Chocolate: www.lindtusa.com
Zingerman's Gourmet Foods:
  www.zingermans.com

SMALL SPACE DISHWASHERS:

GE Spacemaker Dishwasher:
  www.geappliances.com
Miele Slimline Dishwasher: www.miele.com

GENTLE CLEANING PRODUCTS:

Caldrea Home Care: www.caldrea.com
Earth Friendly Products: www.ecos.com
Mrs. Meyer's Clean Day:
  www.mrsmeyers.com
Naturally Yours:
  www.naturallyyoursstore.com

JUST FOR FUN:

Julia Child's Kitchen at the Smithsonian
  Institution: www.americanhistory.si.edu/
  juliachild/default.asp
Easybake Oven Website:
  www.hasbro.com/easybake

C

cabbage. *See* coleslaw; sauerkraut
cabinets. *See* cupboards
cakes
    itty bitty cake, 187–91
    moosehead gingerbread, 192–93
canned soups, 84, 92–94
charcuterie plate, 138
chateaubriand, toaster-oven, 101–2
cheese. *See also* Gorgonzola; Gruyère;
        Parmesan; Roquefort
    chile-cheese corn bread, 163
    mole-style chili nachos, 174
    potato gratin, 159–60
    quiche, 124–27
    stuffed twice-baked potato, 157
chicken
    chicken and rice in a pot, 114–16
    cold chicken plate, 138
    pasta with sage, Parmesan, butter,
        and, 132
    sautéed cutlets Marsala, 117–18
    short-order paella, 116
    summer chicken and rice, 116
    toaster-oven "fried" boneless chicken
        breasts or tenders, 119–20
    toaster-oven poached skinless
        boneless chicken breast, 121
    toaster-oven roasted skinless boneless
        chicken thighs stuffed with ham,
        Gruyère, and sage, 122–23
chile-cheese corn bread, 163
chili, mole-style, 172–73
    baked potato stuffed with, 174
    with black beans, 173–74
    burrito with, 175
    "lasagna," with corn tortillas, 175
    nachos with, 174

chocolate
    ganache frosting, 190–91
    one-pot, no-mess toaster-oven
        brownies, 184–85
choucroute garni, 178–80
clam chowder, improved, 94
claustrophobia, 44–46
cleaning, 20–29, 204–17
    blenders, 83
    dishwashing, 40, 206–12
    floors, 29, 215
    homemade cleaning compounds,
        216–17
    toaster ovens, 110
clutter, 53–54
    dealing with, 11–19, 35, 49, 213
    space-hogging equipment, 60–61
cold plates, 137–39
coleslaw, real German, 168–69
composed salads, 140–43
cookbook holder, 77
corn bread, one-pot, no-mess, 162–63
"couch potato" stuffed baked potato,
    158
countertops, 32, 35, 213, 217
couscous, instant, 164
croutons, 87, 143
cucumber salad, wilted, 170
Cumberland sauce, quick, 152–53
cupboards and shelves, 33–34, 35–37,
    213
    doors, 48, 50
    food storage, 40–41
    lighting, 47–48
    lining shelves, 22
curried mayonnaise, 150
cutlery. *See* flatware; knives

garbage and recyclables, 42–43
garlic, pasta with oil, anchovy, and,
   133–34
German cold cut plate, 138
German coleslaw, real, 168–69
gingerbread, moosehead, 192–93
glassware, 55–56
Gorgonzola, "couch potato" stuffed
   baked potato with, 158
gratin, potato, 159–60
Gruyère, toaster-oven roasted skinless
   boneless chicken thighs stuffed
   with ham, sage, and, 122–23

H

ham
   choucroute garni, 178–80
   homemade split pea soup with, 85–86
   potato gratin, 159–60
   quiche, 124–27
   skillet ham steak, with or without
     egg, 105
   stuffed twice-baked potato with, 157
   toaster-oven roasted skinless boneless
     chicken thighs stuffed with
     Gruyère, sage, and, 122–23
   toaster-oven shirred eggs with, 80
herring plate, 138
hot plates, 27

I

Internet resources, 220
Irish stew, stovetop, 103–4
itty bitty cake, 187–91

K

knives, 64–65

L

lamb
   Scotch broth, Irish style, 104
   stovetop Irish stew, 103–4
   toaster-oven lamb chops, 111
"lasagna," mole-style chili, with corn
   tortillas, 175
lighting, 46–48
low heat cooking, 177

M

mail-order resources, 220
main courses, 95. *See also* chicken; fish;
   pasta; turkey; *specific meats*
   cold plates, 137–39
   composed dinner salads, 140–43
   fish and shrimp dishes, 144–47
   meat dishes, 96–113
   pasta, 128–36
   poultry dishes, 114–23
   quiche, 124–27
Marsala, sautéed cutlets with,
   117–18
marzipan baked apple, 182–83
mayonnaise, 149–50
meat, 96–113. *See also specific meats*
meat loaf
   cold meat loaf plate, 139
   toaster-oven meat loaf, 96–98
microwave ovens, 25, 28
microwave recipes
   baked potato, 155
   baked sweet potato, 156

potato gratin, 159–60
roast boneless center-cut loin of pork,
112–13
roasted skinless boneless chicken
thighs stuffed with ham, 122–23
shirred eggs, 80
stuffed twice-baked potato, 157
toaster ovens, 24, 26–27, 110
tomato sauce
big batch ragù, 176–77
tortellini in broth, 89
tortillas, mole-style chili "lasagna" with,
175
tuna
niçoise salad, 140–41
tuna and white bean "emergency"
salad, 141–42
turkey
pasta with sage, Parmesan, butter,
and, 132
sautéed cutlets Marsala, 117–18

U
utensils, 56–58
knives, 64–65
space hogs, 60–61
storage, 37–39, 50–51

V
veal
mole-style chili, 172–73
toaster-oven meat loaf, 96–98

W
walls, design tips, 48
walnuts, endive salad with Roquefort
and, 166
watercress "stealth salad," 167
windows, cleaning, 217